TWAYNE'S WORLD AUTHORS SERIES

A Survey of the World's Literature

Sylvia Bowman, Indiana University

GENERAL EDITOR

GERMANY

Ulrich Weisstein, Indiana University

EDITOR

Paul Celan

(TWAS 262)

Paul Celan *1920-70*

By JERRY GLENN

University of Cincinnati

Twayne Publishers, Inc. :: New York

To S.G.G. and E.M.M.

Preface

Paul Celan is generally considered to be the most accomplished German-speaking lyric poet to emerge in recent decades. His work is difficult, and various interpretations of his lyrics have been put forward by critics. I personally believe that his poems are intensely emotional and often deeply, if not patently, personal. Celan's experiences as a Jew living in Europe during the Hitler years constitute the single most important theme in his work, and his poems can be truly understood only from this perspective. Celan's most famous poem is "Todesfuge" ("Fugue of Death"), which in surrealistic but unmistakable images describes life and death in a concentration camp. The poem's central image, that of the smoke of the cremated Jewish bodies rising into the air, recurs again and again in the later poetry. Contrary to the opinion of many critics, the emotional basis of "Todesfuge," if not its directness of expression, is quite typical of Celan's work as a whole. Although the poems do, for the most part, speak for themselves, frequent references to Celan's biography and to the historical situation are made throughout the present study. This is done solely for the purpose of illustrating and supporting my interpretation of the emotional content of the poems, regarding which critical opinion is far from unanimous. While I have tried to make the individual interpretations as self-sufficient as possible, it was in many cases impossible to avoid references to other poems by Celan and to explanations of concepts given elsewhere in this study.

This is the first monograph on Celan in English and the first comprehensive survey of his works to appear in any language; all of the previous books devoted to him in German have been concerned with specific aspects of his work. Celan very rarely spoke about his life or his works, and, accordingly, direct autobiographical data are rare. By means of interviews with the people who knew Celan in Vienna in 1948, I have been able to make a tentative reconstruction of his personality at that time. It is still too early to attempt a similar reconstruction concerning his later years. Toward the end of his life Celan was certainly unstable and perhaps mentally ill, and his marriage was becoming increasingly unhappy. That much is certain. The people who are in a position to supply biographical details of his later years are, for understandable reasons, unwilling to do so at the present time.

One sizable and significant body of Celan's work is not treated in this study: his poetic translations into German of the works of many of the greats of world literature. In addition to scores of poems in various anthologies and periodicals, Celan published, as independent books, translations of selected works of such authors as Osip Mandelshtam, Jules Supervielle and William Shakespeare. Practically no scholarly investigations of Celan's translation techniques or of the relationship between his own poetry and that of the poets translated by him have been undertaken, and it is impossible to make an assessment of his translations at the present time.

Until recently, relatively little of Celan's work in translation was available to the American reader. Some selections have been published in various anthologies and periodicals, but only in 1971 did a representative sampling in book form appear. This book of poetic translations, *Speech-Grille,* has been favorably received by reviewers and can be recommended as an admirable, if not unambiguously successful, attempt to render Celan's extremely difficult verse in English.

The translations offered in the present book are literal and are my own. All quotations from German critics and poets are likewise given in my own translation. The Bible is cited according to the King James Version. However, when the text of the standard German translation—that of Luther—is significant, the German phrase is given in brackets. Celan surely knew the Luther Bible; but a detailed study of his knowledge of various Bible texts, Jewish, Catholic, and Protestant, has not yet been undertaken. Throughout the book, the following abbreviations have been used: SU for *Der Sand aus den Urnen* (Vienna: Sexl, 1948); MG for *Mohn und Gedächtnis* (Stuttgart: Deutsche Verlags-Anstalt, 1952); SS for *Von Schwelle zu Schwelle* (Stuttgart: Deutsche Verlags-Anstalt, 1955); SG for *Sprachgitter* (Frankfurt: S. Fischer, 1959); NR for *Die Niemandsrose* (Frankfurt: S. Fischer, 1963); AW for *Atemwende* (Frankfurt: Suhr-

Preface

kamp, 1967); FS for *Fadensonnen* (Frankfurt: Suhrkamp, 1968); LZ for *Lichtzwang* (Frankfurt: Suhrkamp, 1970); SP for *Schnee- part* (Frankfurt: Suhrkamp, 1971); and "Mer" for *Der Meridian. Rede anläßlich der Verleihung des Georg-Büchner-Preises,* quoted from the *Jahrbuch der Deutschen Akademie für Sprache und Dichtung* 1960 (Heidelberg: Lambert Schneider, 1961).

Many individuals and institutions have aided me in the com- pletion of this study. I am especially grateful to the following persons who graciously granted me personal interviews in August and September, 1971, and in many instances placed documents and other materials at my disposal:

Otto Basil. An Austrian poet, editor of *Plan,* where Celan's first poems appeared, and personal friend of Celan.

Milo Dor. An Austrian writer who was one of Celan's closest friends in 1948-1949 and also in later years; and who was instrumental in organizing the Austrian writers' defense of Celan in the Goll affair.

Reinhard Federmann. An Austrian writer who was quite close to Celan in the 1950's.

Claire Goll. The widow of Yvan Goll and herself a poet; in 1960 she publicly accused Celan of plagiarism.

Hermann Hakel. An Austrian writer and editor, and an expert on Jewish literature and traditions; spent five years in a con- centration camp.

Edgar and Erika Jené. A Surrealist painter and his wife who befriended Celan in Vienna in 1948; Jené's paintings were an important influence on Celan.

(Unless otherwise stated, quotations ascribed to the persons just named are from my transcription of the recorded interview.)

I would also like to thank the following persons who answered my written questions in great detail:

Rose Ausländer. A poet and native of Czernowitz; was in close contact with Celan from 1943 to 1947 (letter of Jan. 11, 1972).

Klaus Demus. An Austrian poet who was with Celan in Paris in 1949-1950, when the latter met the Golls (letter of Dec. 13, 1971).

Edith Silbermann. A native of Czernowitz and a long-time friend of Celan's family; now a Germanist and translator in Germany (letter of Jan. 6, 1972).

I am also indebted to many friends and colleagues who have

discussed my interpretations with me, especially Erhard Friedrichsmeyer, Wolfram Mauser, Jakob and Elizabeth Petuchowski, Guy Stern, and to my editor, Ulrich Weisstein, who gave me many helpful suggestions. Of course I do not wish to imply that any of the individuals named above agree with any specific interpretation or conclusion unless this is explicitly stated; some would agree with much of my argument, others probably with very little.

Finally, I am grateful to Annette Smith for patient assistance in typing and transcribing material, to Ivar Ivask, editor of *Books Abroad,* for granting permission to reprint the interpretation of "Mandorla" which originally appeared in his journal; to the Taft fund of the University of Cincinnati, which defrayed the costs of traveling in Europe; to Celan's publishers, Deutsche Verlags-Anstalt, S. Fischer, and Suhrkamp, as well as to Madame Gisèle Celan-Lestrange, for granting permission to quote his poems, and, last but not least, to my wife Sheila, who by right should be given recognition as co-author.

JERRY GLENN

Cincinnati, Ohio

Contents

Chronology

1920   On November 23 Paul Celan born in Czernowitz, Romania, the only child of Leo and Friederike Antschel.

1938   Celan receives his high school diploma. Studies medicine in Tours, France.

1939   Returns to Czernowitz, where he begins to study Romance languages and literatures at the local university.

1940   Czernowitz becomes part of the Soviet Union.

1941   Occupation of Czernowitz by Axis forces. Ghetto.

1942   Deportation of Celan's parents to a concentration camp, where they were to die. Celan manages to escape death, but is put into a work camp.

1943   Returns to Czernowitz, now occupied by Russian troops.

1945   Works as an editor and translator in Bucharest.

1947   In May his first published poems appear in the Romanian journal *Agora*. The poet assumes the pen name "Paul Celan," which he retains for the rest of his life. In December he departs for Vienna.

1948   From January 15 to July 19 Celan is in Vienna. In February his first poems are published in the West in *Plan*. In July he moves to Paris, which is to remain his home. Begins formal study of German literature in Paris. First book of poems: *Der Sand aus den Urnen*. First important essay: "Edgar Jené und Der Traum vom Traume."

1949   Meets Yvan and Claire Goll in November. First major translation into German: Jean Cocteau, *Der goldene Vorhang. Brief an die Amerikaner.*

1950   Receives degree in German. Marries Gisèle Lestrange. First lyric translations in the periodical *Surrealistische Publikationen*.

1952   In May reads his poems at the conference of the Gruppe 47 in Niendorf. Second book of poems: *Mohn und Gedächtnis*.

1955   Third book of poems: *Von Schwelle zu Schwelle*.

1957   Receives the prize of the "Kulturkreis im Bundesverband der deutschen Industrie."

1958   Awarded the literary prize of the city of Bremen.

1959   Fourth collection of poems: *Sprachgitter*.

1960   Only piece of prose fiction: "Gespräch im Gebirg," in the periodical *Die Neue Rundschau*. Awarded the Georg Büchner prize, and important speech, *Der Meridian,* is made upon the occasion of its acceptance.

1963 Fifth collection of poems: *Die Niemandsrose.*

1964 Awarded the literary prize of Nordrhein-Westfalen.

1965 Publication of *Atemkristall* in a limited edition.

1967 Publication of *Atemwende.*

1968 Becomes co-editor of the periodical *L'Ephemère.* Publication of two books of poetry: *Fadensonnen* and the limited edition *Todtnauberg.*

1969 Publication of *Schwarzmaut,* a limited edition. Trip to Israel.

1970 In April drowns in the Seine, an apparent suicide. Publication of *Lichtzwang,* a collection of poems.

1971 Posthumous publication of the collection *Schneepart.*

CHAPTER 1

Introduction

I Paul Celan the Person

PRACTICALLY no information regarding Celan's family or early years is available, and most of the important known facts relating to the poet's life are given in the chronological table. He was very close to his mother, as one sees from his poems, although he rarely mentioned her in conversations with friends. He apparently felt some hostility toward his father, about whom he occasionally spoke. The father, on the other hand, is practically never mentioned in the poetry. As though it were a matter of principle, Celan never spoke of his experiences during the war. He was not in a concentration camp as such, although he spent some time in a work camp doing forced labor. The following brief autobiographical comment, which he sent to the editor of the periodical *Die Wandlung* in connection with the publication of some poems in 1949 (the first of his poems to be published in Germany) indicates his attitude toward his wartime experience: "With the exception of a one-year stay in France, I, for all practical purposes, never left my native city prior to 1941. I don't need to relate what the life of a Jew was like during the war years."[1] It goes without saying that Celan was greatly affected by his experiences during the Nazi years, and it will be necessary to speculate on the effects of these years, as reflected in his writings, in the course of the present study.

His native city, Czernowitz, was occupied by Soviet troops in 1943 as the Germans were pushed back along the Eastern front. Celan left Czernowitz in 1945 for Bucharest, where he worked as an editor and translator. In 1947 he decided to leave Bucharest, probably because of the oppressive nature of the Stalinist regime; his writing hardly qualified as Socialist Realism. In January, 1948, he arrived in Vienna with some twenty to twenty-five poems

15

and a number of letters of introduction from Alfred Margul-Sperber, one of the leading Romanian literary figures. One of these letters was addressed to Otto Basil, the editor of *Plan,* the foremost Viennese literary periodical of the first postwar years. Almost immediately upon his arrival in Vienna, Celan went to Basil, who was very impressed by the young poet and his work. Together Basil and Celan selected seventeen poems for publication in *Plan,* omitting "Todesfuge," among others, because of its excessive length. These poems were published in February, 1948, in the last issue of Basil's journal. Through Basil, Celan was introduced to the most important literary and artistic figures in Vienna, including the surrealist painter Edgar Jené. Jené's paintings made a lasting impression upon Celan, as can be seen in Celan's essay "Edgar Jené und der Traum vom Traume." Celan became known to the Viennese literary public and gave a public reading of his poems that was well attended and received. With the help of Jené and Basil, a small publishing house was found which agreed to publish a volume of Celan's poetry. Primarily through the efforts of Jené, funds were raised to underwrite the costs of publication. Shortly after the book appeared, the author expressed dissatisfaction with it, citing especially the presence of several typographical errors, and ordered it to be recalled.

Although Celan was to some extent able to establish himself as a poet, the economic realities of postwar Vienna proved more difficult to overcome, and in July, 1948, he moved to Paris, where he hoped to be able to earn a living and make a fresh start in life. He studied German literature and received a degree in 1950. In the same year he married a young artist, Gisèle Lestrange. He lived as a writer and translator in Paris, where he also taught German at the Ecole Normale Supérieure. One son, Eric, was born some five years later. Celan received his first important boost toward fame in 1952, when he was still practically unknown in Germany. His Austrian friends Milo Dor and Reinhard Federmann secured an invitation for him to attend the meeting of the Gruppe 47, an informal organization of young writers who met periodically to read and criticize each others' works. Celan read several of his poems and was accorded a generally favorable reception. A major German publisher was impressed by Celan's work and brought out a book of his poems,

Mohn und Gedächtnis, which immediately catapulted the poet into the literary limelight.

Celan never managed to attain financial security, and in addition he suffered increasingly from various anxieties, especially from a fear of anti-Semitism. This fear, variously described as a persecution complex or, especially later in his life, as some form of mental illness, cannot be defined exactly at the present time. It was certainly an abnormal condition which grew worse with the passing of time and contributed in some way to his suicide. At times he saw anti-Semitism and Nazis or neo-Nazis everywhere. The growing power of a right-wing political party in Germany in the 1960's contributed to his fear. Surely the most fully documented illustration of Celan's problem was the "Goll affair." Another of the literary figures to whom Margul-Sperber had written a letter of introduction was Yvan Goll, and in November, 1949, Celan visited the older poet, who was dying of leukemia in a Paris hospital. Goll and his wife Claire quickly befriended Celan, but sometime after Goll's death in 1950 a break occurred between Celan and the widow. Claire Goll accused Celan of personal disloyalty and, later, of literary plagiarism. Celan, in turn, reacted with increasing bitterness, even refusing to allow his poems to be printed in anthologies which were to contain contributions by Yvan Goll. The lack of rationality is evident. Whatever the cause or causes of the personal feud between Celan and Claire Goll, most certainly Yvan Goll never offended Celan in any way. Almost to a man, scholars and poets in Austria, and to a lesser extent in Germany, came to the support of Celan, some even going so far as to maintain that Yvan Goll had plagiarized from Celan.[2] The unfortunate affair was never allowed to abate, and until his death Celan maintained a feeling of animosity toward Claire Goll and apparently even toward her dead husband.

Claire Goll's attack, begun in 1952, was intensified and made public in 1960 in a short article published in the magazine *Baubudenpoet.*[3] The accusation was based primarily on verbal similarities between the unpublished poems of Yvan Goll, to which Celan had access in 1949-1950, and certain poems in *Mohn und Gedächtnis* (1952). The charges seemed to be completely unjustified since many of Celan's poems had already appeared in *Der Sand aus den Urnen* (1948), before Celan met

Goll. But some of the phrases and images cited by Claire Goll had appeared in poems published by her husband in the 1930's and 1940's, and it is possible that Celan was familiar with them. Probably the most important of the phrases mentioned by Claire Goll is the opening image of "Todesfuge," "Black milk of dawn, we drink it...," and the true nature of the entire controversy can be gauged if the various ramifications of this image are examined. On February 1, 1942, Goll published a French poem in the exile newspaper *La Voix de France*. The poem contained the lines "we drink the black milk of the cow of misery," and similar phraseology appears in other poems by Goll from this period. It is possible that Celan knew of Goll's use of the image prior to the composition of "Todesfuge" in 1945.[4] But the image is by no means original with Goll. James K. Lyon cites a passage from Rimbaud with similar wording, as does Peter Mayer, who adds a reference to a poem by Rose Ausländer, written in the early 1930's and published in Czernowitz in 1939, containing the phrase "with black milk."[5] Another possible source is Alfred Margul-Sperber's collection of poems, *Geheimnis und Verzicht*, also published in Czernowitz in 1939, which contains images such as "we drink of the dark milk" (p. 23) and "the milk of evening runs down the dark stalks" (p. 43). The point in question is clearly not plagiarism, but rather the exact nature of literary relationships.

The beginning of the feud can undoubtedly be traced to 1950 when Celan translated a book of Yvan Goll's French poetry, *Chansons Malaises*, into German. When the translation was rejected by the publisher because it was too free, Celan was offended and a quarrel somehow arose between him and Claire Goll. The details are not clear, but the mutual animosity seems to have developed out of this incident.[6] Claire Goll felt that Celan displayed a definite lack of gratitude for the kindness which she and her husband—both important and respected literary figures—offered to the unknown young poet, and she became embittered when Celan's poetry got to be better known than that of her husband.

Yvan Goll certainly was a part of the literary tradition on which Celan draws, and he may even have exerted a direct influence on Celan. But Claire Goll's unfortunate choice of the legal term "plagiarism" undoubtedly served to intensify the emotional reaction of those who came to Celan's defense. Claire Goll had a good point: Celan was writing in the same tradition of German-Jewish poetry as her husband, and this fact, as well as any possible direct influence, was being completely ignored by the critics. But because of the intensity of her attack it is understandable that Celan and his supporters counterattacked with such vigor. Claire Goll must have received poor advice and unwise support from acquaintances and associates prior to launching the attack. The identity of these people, as well as their motives, remains unknown, however.

During my interviews with the poet's friends and acquaintances it became clear to me that Celan was, by any measure, a difficult person. He often broke off friendships for reasons which seem trivial, or even petty. Yet his friends and acquaintances feel a deep sense of loyalty to him, and he was obviously a person to whom one could become deeply attached. Hans Mayer, a noted scholar who was also personally acquainted with Celan, has offered an explanation of this aspect of his personality, which also elucidates certain aspects of Celan's poetry: "It is obvious that nothing which this man and poet ever experienced, read, saw or thought was ever forgotten. . . . The death camps and an insignificant slight from later years alike; he constantly remained aware of everything."[7] This is true of his personal relationships, and can also be seen in his poetry. Celan always exercised extreme care in selecting each word, and his images accordingly contain a multiplicity of references, one of which is often related to the fate of the Jews under Hitler. It seems certain that Celan suffered from a burden of personal guilt dating from a specific event which took place during the war. Many people who were close to him allude to this possibility. It is likely that he confided in two or three friends, and perhaps, someday, the exact nature of the problem will become known; but at present no details are available. The event was undoubtedly similar—in degree of emotional intensity, if not in detail—to an experience related by the novelist Elie Wiesel. In *Night*, an autobiographical novel, Wiesel tells how, as a teenager in a concentration camp, he failed to respond to a call by his father who had been sick for some time. Wiesel reports that the father died that night while he himself was asleep and adds:

They must have taken him away before dawn and carried him to the crematory. He may still have been breathing. There were no prayers at his grave. No candles were lit to his memory. His last word was my name. A summons, to which I did not respond.[8]

The details in Celan's case would, of course, have to be different, but he definitely experienced something of this magnitude which remained with him until his death. Critics often detect subtle indications of guilt in certain of Celan's poems, corroborating the hypothesis of an actual sense of guilt related to his wartime experiences.

II   *Celan and the Critics*

The first two substantial critical works dealing with Celan were the dissertation of Johannes Firges and a chapter of the dissertation of James Lyon, which appeared in 1959 and 1962 respectively.[9] Both works established the importance of key words and images in Celan's poetry and stressed the necessity of interpreting Celan's poems from the perspective of the entire body of his published works. These pioneering studies are excellent in many respects; in fact, they are so persuasive that, for the most part, interpreters of Celan have been reluctant to move away from the ground covered in them. Lyon's study concentrates on nature imagery and interprets many poems in terms of the poetic process and the difficulty of writing poetry today. Subsequent critics have emulated many of his perceptive interpretations, but most have ignored one of his statements made in a discussion of an obviously personal poem: "I suspect many other poems contain personal elements, including some of those interpreted above. Even poems interpreted as dealing with the creative process admit other possibilities of interpretation, and I would willingly accept them."[10]

A few critics have stressed the personal, emotional basis of Celan's poetry, especially Peter Paul Schwarz and Siegbert Prawer.[11] Very recently the great importance of the Jewish element has received detailed attention, especially on the part of Peter Mayer and Joachim Schulze.[12] These two critics have gathered valuable information, and their studies conclusively demonstrate the presence of Judaic themes throughout Celan's works. Mayer also stresses the importance of personal elements: "His quest for his own Jewishness acquired a painful urgency because of the death of his parents and millions of Jews."[13] Mayer's assessment is corroborated by people who knew Celan. Rose Ausländer, for example, maintains that Celan "had a passionately affirmative relationship with Judaism until his death." Klaus Demus, who agrees that Celan felt very strongly about his Jewish heritage, stresses the complexity and individuality of his attitude toward it: "His relation to Judaism was personal, individual and highly complex. . . . He often said to me that although his father was orthodox he had to struggle for his own relation to Judaism." I feel that a changing attitude toward Judaism can be seen in the poems. A direct confrontation, such as that presented in "Todesfuge," yields to less direct expressions in other poems from *Mohn und Gedächtnis*, and many poems from the 1950's seem to point to a withdrawal from at least the unpleasant aspects of the Jewish past. But in 1959 a conscious turning to Jewish themes is seen in "Gespräch im Gebirg," and the poems of *Die Niemandsrose* (1963) are openly and aggressively Jewish.

In their valuable studies, both Mayer and Schulze tend to interpret Celan much too optimistically and affirmatively. Although he respected Judaism and its heritage and tradition, Celan certainly did not believe in a traditional God and had at best ambivalent feelings toward many aspects of the Jewish religion. Mayer and Schulze compare Celan with such Jewish thinkers of an older generation as Franz Rosenzweig (1886-1929), Martin Buber (1878-1965), and Hermann Cohen (1842-1918), finding in Celan, as in these older writers, a fairly traditional interpretation of Judaism and its historical significance. Mayer, for example, cites Cohen's book *Religion der Vernunft* (*The Religion of Reason*), which maintains that suffering "is preparation for salvation."[14] Such a view is alien to Celan, as it was alien to many Jews after 1945. Celan's sharp rejection of reason in "Edgar Jené und der Traum vom Traume," which will be discussed below, is a strong indication of his rejection of such positions as the one taken by Cohen. Celan's relation to Hassidism—a form of Jewish mysticism popularized by Buber—is ambivalent, as is his attitude toward Buber's original writings. He rejected certain optimistic aspects of both, while retaining a sincere respect for other facets. Similarly, many critics mention Job, who after much patient suffering is returned to God's favor,

as an important prototype for Celan's poetry. But the salvation
with which the Book of Job concludes is missing in Celan,
and a much better comparison can be made with Ahasver, the
Wandering Jew. Mayer has accurately noted this relationship:
"The Eternal Jew [as he is called in German], the Wandering
Jew became images of his poetry."[15]

The Wandering Jew is indeed an appropriate symbol for
Celan's interpretation of the Jewish fate. The Jews remained
outcasts for centuries while retaining, for the most part, their
sense of identity as a people and their faith in the eventual fulfillment of the promises of redemption and salvation which had
been made to them by God. The systematic persecution by the
Nazis changed the attitude of many Jews. The following remark
by an inmate of a concentration camp quoted by Elie Wiesel,
is certainly indicative of this fact and can probably be considered typical to some extent: "I've got more faith in Hitler than
in anyone else. He's the only one who's kept his promises, all his
promises, to the Jewish people."[16]

There are, of course, many different kinds of reactions by
Jews who survived the Nazi years in Central Europe. Celan
practically never spoke directly about the war years and his
experiences at that time, but I feel that a definite and consistent
attitude, resulting from these experiences, is reflected in his
poetry and is often overlooked by critics. Celan's attitude seems
closely to resemble that of Elie Wiesel, a Jewish writer who has
not been reluctant to speak directly of his emotions and attitudes. Wiesel, a Jew born in the same general region as Celan
and roughly his contemporary, was sent to a concentration camp,
by some miracle managed to survive and, like Celan, settled in
Paris and began to write. Although he knew no French at the
conclusion of the war, he learned the language and now writes
in it, avoiding German, the language of the Nazis.

Wiesel's autobiographical novel *Night* offers views which,
mutatis mutandis, Celan might also have expressed:

For the first time, I felt revolt rise up in me. Why should I bless
His name? The Eternal, Lord of the Universe, the All-Powerful and
Terrible, was silent. What had I to thank Him for? . . . Never shall
I forget that night, the first night in camp, which has turned my
life into one long night. . . . Never shall I forget those flames which
consumed my faith forever.[17]

In his works Wiesel consistently displays an attitude of hatred toward the Germans and toward Germany. He describes, for example, his first trip to Germany which took place in 1962. He tells of the hate and repulsion he felt when speaking to the Germans, and how he nonetheless remained extremely polite in his speeches. He says that he hated himself for being unable to express his hate directly to the Germans; he hated himself for his obsequious politeness when he wanted to express his utter contempt for Germany. Wiesel concludes his essay describing his trip to Germany as follows: "Every Jew, somewhere in his being, should set apart a zone of hate—healthy, virile hate— for what the German personifies and for what persists in the German. To do otherwise would be a betrayal of the dead. I shall not return to Germany soon again."[18]

Another aspect of the problem which seems to be reflected, and paralleled, in Celan is the association of Christianity with the Nazis. Perhaps the most direct expression of this attitude can be found in Richard Rubenstein: "In one area the Nazis took Christianity very seriously. They did not invent a new villain. They took over the two-thousand-year-old Christian tradition of the Jew as villain. . . . The roots of the death camps must be sought in the mythic structure of Christianity."[19] Hermann Hakel expresses a similar attitude: "Whatever is Catholic is anti-Semitic, the two go hand in hand. The Church cannot live without us [Jews], even if only as an enemy; it must have us, be it to burn us or to baptize us." Many Christians have, of course, over the years admitted the problem and attempted to effect a change. For example, in 1933 Conrad Moehlmann published a book entitled *The Christian-Jewish Tragedy*. In his preface he writes: "Some Christian had to write this book. An apology to Judaism on the part of Christianity has long been overdue." The lack of success of such attempts at reform is made clear when the conclusion of Moehlmann's preface—ironically dated Good Friday, 1933—is read today: "As we write, the Hitler regime promulgates enactment after enactment indirectly or directly concerned with the Jews of Germany. May Germany's Jews be spared further suffering and the Christian-Jewish tragedy not be heightened thereby."[20]

Celan most assuredly shared the attitudes expressed by Hakel and Rubenstein and felt extremely bitter about the Germans

and about Christianity because of the role each played in the
attempted extermination of the Jews under Hitler. Direct ex-
presssions of this view, or of any other emotional stance, are
practically nonexistent in Celan. An anecdote, related by Reinhard Federmann will, however, illustrate Celan's attitudes and
his bitter and ironic mode of expression. Federmann reports:

I met Paul Celan again in 1952 at a meeting of the Gruppe 47 in
Niendorf. After the meeting the participants traveled as a group
to Hamburg . . . and the writers who lived there . . . availed themselves of this opportunity to show us St. Pauli. So two or three dozen
of us were walking along the Reeperbahn one evening. I was walking
next to Celan and we were engaged in a conversation. Suddenly
a great commotion arose on the street. A woman in a Volkswagen
had run over a dog which had managed to break away from its
owner. The two women cried, "O my goodness! I didn't mean to do
that." — "O my goodness, what have you done!" And then Celan
turned to me and said, "See how they carry on—about a dog" [Bei
einem *Hund*—jammern sie].

That two German women would cry about a dog which had
been run over elicited an ironic comment from Celan, who was
immediately reminded that several million Jews had been killed
without any such reaction on the part of the Germans. Like Elie
Wiesel he felt a deep hatred of the Germans, but unlike Wiesel
he was unwilling or unable to express this emotion directly.

The combination of Celan's hostile attitude toward Germany
and Christianity and his ambivalent attitude toward Judaism,
on the one hand, and his inability to forget anything, on the
other, has produced some striking effects in his poetry. Celan's
poems contain countless allusions to the Bible, to other
poets, to his own poems from earlier years, and even to
scholarly literature, and these references often express, indirectly, his feelings of hostility. Two very common sources of
such allusions are the beginning of Genesis, "And the Spirit of
God moved upon the face of the waters. And God said, let there
be light . . . ," and the first chapter of the gospel according to St.
John, "In the beginning was the Word, and the Word was with
God, and the Word was God. . . . In him was life; and the life
was the light of men. . . . And the Word was made Flesh." From
a theological point of view, both the God of Genesis and of
John are rejected by Celan. The primacy of the "Word" ("logos")

in the New Testament implies a denial of the "Spirit" (Hebrew "Ruach," "breath") of Genesis. While I was discussing Genesis with Hermann Hakel, the "logos" of John was mentioned and Hakel replied: "But you won't find that in our [Jewish] writings ... don't hold me responsible for the *logos;* I'm no goi," indicating an immediate, almost instinctive awareness of the distinction, and of its significance for Jew and Gentile. Celan surely shared this consciousness. The ascendancy of Christianity may, accordingly, be implied by the "word," and this and other elements of John's gospel receive ironic treatment in Celan's poetry. Celan, for example, often constructs elaborate word plays on the different meanings of "logos" and "word." The reader must continually be aware that words may have many different meanings and that two or more of these are often present in the poetry. Celan read incessantly and regularly consulted such reference tools as etymological dictionaries—in addition to the Bible and works of literature—in composing his carefully-worded verse.

A specific technique favored by Celan utilizes many of the features discussed above. Since reference will frequently be made to it in the course of the present study, a brief explanation is necessary here. The technique consists of an allusion—often extended over several lines or even through an entire poem—to a religious or literary work or works, for the purpose of denying or poetically "refuting" the work in question. Typically one of Celan's poems will allude to the theme and vocabulary of both a literary work and a Biblical passage, by means of a series of verbal echoes and even direct quotations. The literary work generally expresses some form of optimism and affirmation, which is contradicted in Celan's poem, often by means of irony. This process was first described by Götz Wienold in an excellent article which explained its use in the poem "Tenebrae."[21] Wienold referred to the technique as a "Widerruf," and since the possible English equivalents for "Widerruf," such as "poetic refutation," are rather awkward, I have retained the German term when making reference to this phenomenon.

In describing the "Widerruf" technique, Wienold points out the bitterly ironic aspects of Celan's poetry. In conclusion he offers a warning, which has unfortunately been largely ignored since its publication in 1968: "One has the impression that critics want to deny the conclusions which the reader must draw from

Celan's poetry; they want to silence the anguished cry of these poems, as they push the poems off into the sphere of aesthetic games." It is my contention that Wienold is absolutely correct. Celan's poems are intensely emotional expressions of anguish. Sometimes he is concerned with the impact of the past upon the present and at other times his concern goes one step further, to his own role as a German-speaking Jewish poet whose dominant theme is this history. Celan rarely writes about poetry or art in the abstract, and his poems are certainly not aesthetic games.

It is especially difficult to analyze the effectiveness, or the artistic merit, of a lyric poet. Celan is certainly no exception, and critics for the most part seem to assume his greatness without attempting to analyze or explain it. I, too, shall in general assume rather than attempt to "prove" the high artistic quality of the poems which I discuss and shall concentrate rather on the multiplicity of meanings of individual words and images, and the tremendous emotional impact of individual poems; in short, on the nature of the extraordinary richness of Celan's poetry. It is, of course, not necessary to recognize all the word plays or Biblical allusions in a given poem in order to feel attracted to it, and in fact some critics and probably most German readers have often been unaware of specific frames of reference in the poems. But a more complete understanding of a poem will invariably facilitate, as well as complement, appreciation of it.

CHAPTER 2

Works in Prose

I "Edgar Jené und der Traum vom Traume"

CELAN published only a small amount of prose, but it is of considerable importance, both in its own right and as an aid in interpreting the poems. In 1948 a poetic essay appeared, following a short preface by Otto Basil, as an introductory text to a book containing reproductions of several of Edgar Jené's paintings and lithographs. The book is exceedingly rare, and Celan's essay, which has never been reprinted, is practically unknown. The interesting and revealing essay is entitled "Edgar Jené und der Traum vom Traume." Seldom does Celan speak as directly as here, and in no other work does he reveal more of himself. The tone of the piece is set at the beginning: "Ich schlug eine Bresche in die Wände und Einwände der Wirklichkeit und stand vor dem Meeresspiegel" ("I hammered a breach in the walls and contradictions of reality and stood before the mirror of the sea"). The word play contained in "Wände" and "Einwände" —walls and objections or contradictions—suggests a lack of hard and fast distinctions between concrete objects and abstract concepts; contradictions are just as "real" as walls, and just as much in need of penetration.

After a short waiting period Celan, like Alice through the looking glass, "followed Edgar Jené down into his pictures." But his eyes were still accustomed to function according to the rules of empirical reality and were therefore unable to give themselves up to the uncontrolled associations by means of which the inner reality of feeling and emotion can be experienced. He nonetheless finds a way to understand the new world which he has entered:

Mein Mund aber, der höher lag als meine Augen und kühner war, weil er oft aus dem Schlaf gesprochen, war mir vorausgeeilt und rief mir seinen Spott zu: . . . "Hol dir lieber ein paar Augen aus

27

dem Grund deiner Seele und setze sie dir auf die Brust: dann
erfährst du, was sich hier ereignet."

(But my mouth, which lay higher than my eyes and was bolder,
because it often has spoken in my sleep, had run ahead of me and
called back its ridicule to me: . . . "You would be better off getting
a pair of eyes from the bottom of your soul and placing them on
your breast: then you will find out what is happening here.")

The values and truths of this realm are not accessible through
the brain and rational analysis. The eyes must, hence, lead
directly to the heart if they are to transmit an accurate image
of this new reality of emotion and intuition. The removal of the
eyes from their normal position suggests physical blindness which
is often paradoxically associated with sight in Celan's poems.

Celan next describes a conversation with a friend concerning
possible ways of restoring a sense of order in the world—an
implicit reference to the question of how one can best come
to terms with the war and the death camps and all their ramifications, personal and philosophical. The friend's approach is
rational and in some respects Freudian; for in his opinion, if the
past is recognized, rationally defined, and then faced, it can be
overcome:

Die Vernunft solle walten, den Worten also den Dingen, Geschöpfen
und Begebenheiten, ihr eigentlicher (primitiver) Sinn wiedergegeben
werden, indem man sie mit dem Königswasser des Verstandes rein-
wusch. Ein Baum sollte wieder ein Baum werden, sein Zweig, an
den man in hundert Kriegen die Empörer geknüpft, ein Blütenzweig,
wenn es Frühling würde.

(Reason should rule [the friend argued], words—that is, things,
creatures, and events—should recover their own (primitive) meaning,
by washing them again with the *aqua fortis* [literally: royal water]
of the intellect. A tree should once again become a tree, its branch,
from which the insurgents of a hundred wars have been hung, should
become a blossoming branch, when spring came.)

The tone of Celan's account of the friend's argument is ironic.
A word play is implied by the word "Blütenzweig"; the branch
which is to bloom was only a short time ago bloody with war,
a "Blut-zweig." Celan then states his objections, which he succinctly bases on the recognition that: ". . . Geschehenes mehr

war als Zusätzliches zu Gegebenem, mehr als ein mehr oder minder schwer entfernbares Attribut des Eigentlichen, sondern ein dieses Eigentliche in seinem Wesen Veränderndes, ein starker Wegbereiter unausgesetzter Verwandlung." ("That which has happened is more than simply an addition to a given condition, more than a characteristic of the essential which may be more or less difficult to remove; it is rather something which changes the very essence of this reality, a powerful forerunner of constant change.") Celan denies that the wrongs of the past can be forgiven and forgotten; each event of the past alters reality, and the present can never be isolated from the effects of past events.

The friend, however, is persistent; he reasserts his belief in the power of reason to improve life and asks: "Wie aber . . . soll das gelingen, wenn du und andere wie du die Tiefe nie verlassen und immerzu Zwiesprache halten mit den finstern Quellen?" ("But how can that ever come about if you and others like you never leave the depths and keep on holding converse with the dark springs?") Celan here identifies one of the objects which he directly addresses in his poetry: the dark springs of the unconscious. They, and only they, constitute reality. The reference to the springs, "Quellen," is significant. "Blut" and "Blüte" can etymologically be traced to the same root, a word meaning "quellen," to flow upwards. By choosing this word, a continuation of, and elaboration upon, the word play implied earlier, Celan offers poetic "proof" of his contention that a blossom on a tree can never be merely a blossom; both because the word "Blüte" suggests "Blut," and because the blossoming tree was but a short time earlier covered with blood. This way of perceiving reality is neither logical nor rational, and hence it is described in images. Ironically, the word "Quellen," like "Blüte," is spoken by the friend. Even though he does not say "blood," the words he uses in his admonition to trust reason conjure up the very associations which he urges Celan to forget. The use of the tree image is based upon traditional symbolic values; in addition to the familiar tree of life, many instances of the tree representing the human sphere in literature and art could be cited. Hence the blossoming and bloody trees suggest happy people and the dead, respectively. As with the trees, any present human happiness automatically brings remembrances of the blood of the past. This passage demonstrates how closely language and historical reality are related in Celan's thought. A poetic definition of cabala, the basis of one important branch of Jewish mysticism, comes to mind: "What is cabala but a fundamental marveling at the magical power of the word?" It is easy to see why Celan so often inverts the positive symbolic and allegorical elements of Jewish mysticism. Formerly God's goodness was revealed in every word and every object. But now only God's absence is seen.

Celan goes on to observe that man is a prisoner of the past:

Ich war mir klar geworden, daß der Mensch nicht nur in den Ketten des äußeren Lebens schmachtete, sondern auch geknebelt war und nicht sprechen durfte—und wenn ich von der Sprache rede, so ist damit die ganze Sphäre menschlicher Ausdrucksmittel gemeint—weil seine Worte (Gebärden und Bewegungen) unter der tausendjährigen Last falscher und entstellter Aufrichtigkeit stöhnten—was war unaufrichtiger als die Behauptung, diese Worte seien irgendo im Grunde noch dieselben!

(It had become clear to me that man not only languished in the chains of external reality, but was also gagged and could not speak —and when I refer to speech, I mean the entire sphere of human communication and expression—because his words (gestures and movements) groaned under the burden of a thousand years of false and distorted sincerity—what was less sincere than the assertion that these words somehow or other had basically remained unchanged!)

Neither the actual blossom nor the word "Blüte" can have the same significance they had before Hitler. (The reference to "of a thousand years" contains an allusion both to the "Millennium" of Christ and to the phrase "thousand-year empire" used by Hitler to predict the durability of the Nazi regime.)

How might a new beginning be possible? Celan ventures an answer: "Aus den entferntesten Bezirken des Geistes mögen Worte und Gestalten kommen, Bilder und Gebärden, traumhaft verschleiert und traumhaft entschleiert. . . ." ("Words and forms should come from the farthest regions of the spirit, veiled as in a dream and revealed as in a dream.") A new brightness will emerge which can be perceived and comprehended when the senses are reoriented, enabling them to dissolve the distinction between sight, hearing, and touch. A new irrational, unsystematic mode of perception is thereby made possible: "Ich folge meinen wandernden Sinnen in die neue Welt des Geistes und erlebe die Freiheit. Hier, wo ich frei bin, erkenne ich auch, wie arg ich drüben belogen wurde." ("I follow my wandering senses into the new world of the spirit and experience freedom. Here, where I am free, I recognize how badly I have been deceived over there.")

A description and interpretation of four of Jené's pictures follow. The first, which was modelled after a gouache owned by Celan, is entitled "Ein Segel verläßt ein Auge" ("A Sail Leaves an Eye"). In the picture, a female face, in profile, is directed upwards. No pupil can be seen in the eye, and the "sail" is a ship which seems to be floating in a waterfall—tears are suggested —flowing downwards from the eye. The eye is especially important, here, as so often in Celan, and the observer remarks that the sail "...wird heimkehren in die leere und seltsam sehende Augenhöhle" ("will return to the empty and strangely-seeing socket of the eye"). The eye is capable of sight although not in a conventional manner. The face is "ein eisiges Denkmal an den Zugängen des innern Meeres, das auch ein Meer der welligen Tränen ist" ("an icy monument at the entrances to the inner sea, which is also a sea of billowing tears"). Several of Celan's favorite images appear here in close proximity: the eye, tears, the sea, and an icy landscape.

The second picture which Celan discusses is "Der Sohn des Nordlichts" ("The Son of the Northern Lights"). The Northern Lights are traditionally associated with war and Celan builds upon this symbolism.[1] Jené's terrifying painting depicts a fragmented figure with empty eyes which seems to be moving both across and over a surrealistic forest of icy trees: "Da wo der Mensch in den Schneewäldern seiner Verzweiflung in Fesseln erstarrt ist, kommt er groß vorüber." ("There, where man is frozen in the snow-woods of his despair, he [the son of the Northern Lights] awe-inspiring [literally: large] passes by"). His empty eyes command attention: "...sie haben gesehen, was alle gesehen haben, und mehr." ("They have seen what all have seen, and more.") According to Edgar Jené, Celan felt an affinity to this phantom, "Der Sohn des Nordlichts."[2] Within the historical context, the figure certainly suggests the condition of the world—as well as Celan's state of mind—in 1948. But a connection with the more distant past is also suggested in Celan's commentary: "Mehr als einer wird ungläubig bleiben, wenn man ihm vom Sohn des Nordlichts erzählt. Ungläubig auch heute noch, wo doch das Haar der Berenike schon so lange unter den Sternen hängt." ("More than one person will still refuse to believe when he is told about the Son of the Northern Lights. He will not believe, even today, when the Hair of Berenice has been hanging among the stars for such a long time.") The hair of Berenice is the constellation Coma Berenices, named after the wife of the Egyptian king Ptolemy III. Berenice promised a lock of her hair as an offering to Aphrodite when she prayed for the safe return of her husband from the Syrian war. The hair vanished from the temple, and a famous astronomer immediately discovered it in the heavens, transformed into the constellation. The war referred to involved the Jews to some extent and was one of the events leading up to the Maccabean wars; it was a time, according to I Maccabees 1:11 when "evils were multiplied in the earth." Now the hair is a constellation, and stars invariably suggest Jews and Judaism in Celan. Although the connections are far from "logical," Celan seems to be implying that the terror reflected in the painting should not surprise anyone, since the systematic persecution of the Jews has a tradition dating back to the time of the discovery of the constellation Coma Berenices.

Celan makes a slight change in the title of the next picture, "Ein rotes Meer geht über Land" ("A Red Sea Goes over Land"), which depicts a number of creatures eerily walking across a bloody landscape. He refers to it under the title "Das Blutmeer geht über Land" ("The Blood-Sea Goes over Land"). Here Celan explicitly states his reason for valuing this kind of art so highly: "Was Edgar Jené hier erstmalig Gestalt annehmen läßt—ist es nur hier zuhause? Wollten wir nicht auch den Alp der alten Wirklichkeit besser erkennen, wollten wir nicht den Schrei des Menschen, unseren eigenen Schrei, vernehmen, lauter als sonst, gellender?" ("What Edgar Jené here, for the first time, gives form to—is it only to be found here? Aren't we also able better to recognize the nightmare-spirit of the old reality, aren't we able to hear the scream of man, our own scream, louder than usual, and more piercing?") Reality is both absurd and terrible. It is so terrible, so absurd that it can only be ex-

pressed in images and words which confuse the normal relationship between the senses and which, on the surface, seem to
distort rather than clarify reality.

The final picture described in Celan is "Lasset uns schwören
im Schlafe" ("Let us Swear in Sleep"). It depicts a pillar with
a rounded but slightly irregular object on top, not unlike an
upraised arm and clenched fist. Shadowy figures can be seen
around the base of the column. The text is extremely important,
and no less difficult:

Oft haben wir als Wache geschworen: im heißen Schatten ungeduldiger Fahnen, im Gegenlicht des fremden Todes, am Hochaltar
unserer heiliggesprochenen Vernunft. Und wir haben unsere Schwüre
auch gehalten, um den Preis unseres heimlichen Lebens, aber als
wir dorthin zurückkehrten, wo wir sie geleistet—was mußten wir
sehen? Die Farbe der Fahne war noch dieselbe, der Schatten, den
sie warf, sogar größer als zuvor. Und wieder hob man die Hand
zum Schwur. Aber wem gelobte man jetzt Treue? Dem Anderen,
dem, dem wir Haß geschworen. Und der fremde Tod? Er hatte
recht so zu tun, als hätte es unserer Schwüre überhaupt nicht bedurft
. . . Am Hochaltar endlich stand ein Hahn und krähte . . . Laßt uns
also versuchen, im Schlafe zu schwören.

(We often swore as sentinels [or: while awake]: in the hot shadow
of impatient banners, in the counter-light of the alien death, on the
high altar of our canonized rationality. And we kept our vows, too,
at the price of our secret life, but when we returned to the place
where we had made them—what did we see? The color of the banner
was still the same, and the shadow which it cast was even larger
than before. And again one lifted his hand to make an oath. But
to whom did one now swear fidelity? To the Other, *to that one,* the
one to whom we had pledged our hate. And the alien death? He
was right to act as though our vows had been quite unnecessary . . .
At the high altar, finally, a cock stood and crowed . . . So let us
try to swear in sleep.)

The contrast between reason and feeling is again of central
importance. The reference seems to be to the Jews who formerly
swore allegiance to reason. They expected reasonable behavior
on their part to lead to reasonable behavior on the part of their
enemies. Their religion and traditions are the counter-light—a
word suggesting opposition to the "Light" of the beginning of
the gospel of St. John—and the alien death suggests the death

camps. The Germans, of course, ignored the good will of the Jews; the Nazis, indeed, had no use for these "vows." But it was a false God who had been worshipped. Later, after the war, another oath was sworn. But it is no longer "we," but "one" who takes the oath. This expression is less personal. It alludes to the dehumanizing effect of the camps and also indicates that there is no longer a collective sense of unity among the Jews. Many are dead, and the survivors have different interpretations of what happened, as well as of what must be done now. The "one" accordingly seems to refer to Celan himself and to other unspecified Jews who might share his view. He now lifts his hand to swear allegiance to the opposite of reason, "Let us try to swear in sleep," i.e., let us seek values in that other realm. The cock crowing refers to Peter's denial of Jesus. Now a double denial or betrayal has taken place. Previously the Jews betrayed their Jewishness by cooperating with their enemies, primarily German and Christian. Now they reverse their previous position and deny Christ and the possibility of a reconciliation between the (Christian) Germans and the Jews.

II *Three Short Texts*

Three short prose texts deserve at least brief discussion in this context. In 1958 Celan published a one-page essay in which he discussed his current literary work.[3] In this essay Celan says that he mistrusts the "beautiful," and that he must work with a "grayer" language. But he qualifies his statement. He is not speaking of language as an end, but as a means; language as such is not important, "sondern immer nur ein unter dem besonderen Neigungswinkel seiner Existenz sprechendes Ich, dem es um Kontur und Orientierung geht" ("but always only as an "I" who speaks from the specific perspective of his own existence, and who is concerned with contour and orientation"). Celan's conception of reality remains undefined. It is surely somewhat different from that formulated ten years earlier in "Edgar Jené und der Traum vom Traume." But as before, reality is the important thing, and language is one means, a very important one, of exploring it.

The second text is a letter dated May 18, 1960, and addressed to Hans Bender, in which Celan explains why he is unwilling to write an essay on his own poetry for Bender's anthology *Mein Gedicht ist mein Messer*.[4] After attempting to justify his refusal, Celan poses the question: " 'Wie macht man Gedichte?' " ("How does one make poems?"), a reference to a famous dictum by Gottfried Benn, "Poems very rarely happen—poems are made."[5] Celan comments that "Das Machen über die Mache allmählich zur Machenschaft wird" ("Making, by way of window-dressing, gradually becomes intrigue"). As often, a word play is involved. Celan is playing with the words "Machen" ("to make"), "Mache" ("window-dressing, make-up"), and "Machenschaft" ("intrigue, machinations"); and the word play is an ironic "Widerruf" of Benn's statement. Celan, then, sees the poem not as a product of the poet's handicraft, but as an expression of human emotion. He concludes the letter with an unusually direct statement about his own outlook: "Wir leben unter finsteren Himmeln, und— es gibt wenig Menschen. Darum gibt es wohl auch so wenig Gedichte. Die Hoffnungen, die ich noch habe, sind nicht groß; ich versuche, mir das mir Verbliebene zu erhalten." ("We live under dark skies and—there are few human beings. This is probably the reason why there are so few poems. The hopes which I have are not great; I shall attempt to hold on to what is still left to me.") Celan directly expresses both a very negative philosophy of life and his continuing belief in the existence of an intimate relationship between poem and poet. His poems often corroborate this confession; upon close reading they tend to reveal themselves as personal and emotional, and they more often reveal an attitude of despair than one of hope.

One highly ironic sentence in another short text, a letter addressed to Robert Neumann in which Celan declines to contribute a story to an anthology, is important: "jetzt, beim streng nach Adorno und auch sonst deutsch europäisch denkenden Merkur, weiß man endlich, wo die Barbaren zu suchen sind."[6] ("Now, invoking *Mercury*, which strictly follows Adorno and other German-European lines of thought, one can finally see where the barbarians are to be found.") Celan's reference is to the highly respected periodical *Merkur*, "a German periodical for European thinking," as it characterizes itself, and to the influential German cultural critic Theodor Adorno who has asserted that it is "barbaric" to write poetry after Auschwitz, thereby implicitly calling Celan, who writes such poetry, a

barbarian. Also attacked is the group of critics who find fault
with "Todesfuge" on the grounds that it is too beautiful and,
therefore, in a sense lends dignity to the death camps by trans-
forming them artistically. Celan does not miss the irony inherent
in his being called a barbarian, even by someone who, like
Adorno, spent the war in exile.

III   Two Speeches

There seems to be a great difference between the essays discussed above and Celan's only two public speeches, "Ansprache
anläßlich der Entgegennahme des Literaturpreises der Freien
Hansestadt Bremen" (1958), and Der Meridian (1960), each
made on the occasion of the acceptance of a prestigious literary
prize. The tone, especially of the latter text, seems more ana-
lytical, the arguments are more carefully developed, and the
irony is apparently lacking. Some critics tend to take the speeches
very seriously, as well as literally, and attempt to construct a
theory of poetry from the speeches, a theory to which they then
expect Celan's poems to conform. Horst Bienek noted this phenomenon, with appropriate irony: "A couple of fragments [from
the Meridian speech] torn out of context are circulating, and they
have to serve in place of a systematic theory of poetry."[7] A
close analysis of the speeches reveals that, in fact, Celan's tone
remains basically the same, for the irony and personal involvement are still very much in evidence.

The Bremen speech is quite short, being only two or three
pages in length. The first paragraph sets the tone: "Denken und
Danken sind in unserer Sprache Worte ein und desselben Ur-
sprungs. Wer ihrem Sinn folgt, begibt sich in den Bedeutungs-
bereich von: 'gedenken,' 'eingedenk sein,' 'Andenken,' 'Andacht.'
Erlauben Sie mir, Ihnen von hier aus zu danken."[8] ("Thinking
and thanking have one and the same origin in our language.
Whoever follows their sense comes to the semantic field of:
'remember,' 'be mindful,' 'remembrance,' 'devotion.' Allow me to
thank you from this perspective.") Celan's customary awareness
of word meanings and the significance of their relationships is
easily recognized here. The reference to "our" language, made in
Germany to an audience of Germans, immediately commands
attention. The words he lists refer to his own condition: he

cannot forget, and he must be polite, at least on the surface. He thanks the Germans, in Germany, in German, while thinking of them and of the victims, while being mindful of them and the victims, and while being devoted only to the Jewish dead. The irony of his thanks, from this perspective, is plain indeed.

In the second paragraph, Celan refers to his own background, and then mentions a poem by Rudolf Borchardt (1877-1945), "Ode mit dem Granatapfel," and the man to whom the poem is dedicated, Rudolf Alexander Schröder (1878-1962). Both references are ironic. The poem, written early in the twentieth century, contains the line "we, too, wait following a totally destroyed youth," which appears in the same stanza as the phrase "our autumn day."[9] A reference to a wasted youth by a German born in 1877 (the years 1880 to 1914 were quite prosperous for Germany) must have seemed hollow to a Jew born in 1920, whose youth was truly destroyed. The similarity between Borchardt's word, "vernichtet," and a common word for the death camps, "Vernichtungslager," did not escape Celan, and the presence of the word "autumn"—a personal cipher relating to the death of the poet's mother—heightens the irony. Among the achievements of Rudolf Alexander Schröder, a respected minor poet, are several volumes of very traditional Christian verse and a number of patriotic poems, such as "Deutscher Schwur" ("German Oath"), which contains the following lines: "Holy Fatherland/ In danger,/ Your sons stand/ Prepared to defend you."[10]

Language, Celan continues, was one thing which remained intact after the war, even though it had to "go through" the "thousand darknesses of death-bringing speech." "This" language, which is death-bringing, is German, the language of death, and the only language at his disposal. He uses it but he never forgets its implications: "In dieser Sprache habe ich ... Gedichte zu schreiben versucht, ... um mir Wirklichkeit zu entwerfen." ("In this language I have tried to write poetry, in order to acquire a perspective of reality for myself.") Celan goes on to compare a poem to a letter in a bottle which is cast into the sea and may come to land, "an Herzland vielleicht" ("to heart-land, perhaps"). He then continues: "Gedichte sind auch in dieser Weise unterwegs: sie halten auf etwas zu. Worauf? Auf ... ein ansprechbares Du vielleicht, auf eine ansprechbare

Wirklichkeit." ("Poems are even in this manner under way. They
are heading for something. For what? For . . . a thou which can
be addressed, perhaps, for a reality which can be addressed.")
The thoughts expressed in the last half of the speech are serious
ones; Celan does, indeed, seek reality in his poems. This reality,
however, is bound to his own experiences and to his inability
to free himself from their effects. Poems are sent forth to express
emotions, even if there is no assurance that they will ever reach
a "heart-land" which can accept and understand them.

Celan's longest and most carefully developed essay is *Der
Meridian,* a speech which he made in Darmstadt in 1960 upon
receiving the highly coveted Georg Büchner Prize. In his address Celan follows the tradition, set by previous recipients,
of discussing the works of Georg Büchner (1813-1837), a pro-
gressive, even avant-garde, German writer. He begins by citing,
or rather by alluding to, a passage from Büchner's drama about
the French Revolution, *Dantons Tod*: "Die Kunst, das ist, Sie
erinnern sich, ein marionettenhaftes, jambisch-fünffüßiges und
. . . kinderloses Wesen." ("Art, that is—you remember—a marion-
ette-like, five-beat-iambic, and . . . childless being.") Büchner's
character Camille uses these words in the second act of the drama
as he takes up a theme begun in the previous scene. There
one man speaks of the "technical arts," and, following a few
other remarks, his companion ends the conversation by saying:
"Go to the theater." Camille's first sentence builds upon these
casual statements and initiates a discussion of art. He speaks of
marionettes on a string which speak in iambic pentameter, alluding to the lack of spontaneity in art and implying that men have
just as little freedom as do puppets on a string.

Celan next refers to a passage from another drama by Büchner,
Leonce und Lena, in which a character presents two figures in
masks and observes that they are "nothing but art and mechan-
ism." As Otto Pöggeler has pointed out, Celan is alluding to the
basic meaning of *techne,* the Greek word for art, "a handcraft,
something made";[11] both English and German have closely related words which reflect the two different meanings: "künstlich"
and "künstlerisch," "artificial" and "artistic." Celan is, then, once
again alluding to and disagreeing with Gottfried Benn's conception of poetry as something "made," something merely artificial. In 1951 Benn was the first recipient of the new Büch-

ner prize, and Hans Mayer has perceptively pointed out that: "*The Meridian* was explicitly conceived as a counter-speech. . . . The poetic theory of the Meridian is an answer from the year 1960 to Gottfried Benn's speech of 1951."[12] It is the removal of the human element, characteristic of Benn's formulation, with which Celan is taking issue. The passage from *Leonce und Lena*, to an even greater degree than that from *Dantons Tod*, is using the image of the mechanical aspects of art to suggest man's lack of freedom; so often man is forced to function like a robot, as though he had no freedom of choice whatsoever.

But one character in *Dantons Tod*, Celan then points out, refuses to accept her role as robot, as puppet. She is Lucile, the wife of Camille. Camille is executed, dying, as Celan observes, a "theatrical, one might even say iambic, death." Lucile then mounts the platform and screams, in the presence of a group of revolutionaries, "Es lebe der König!" ("Long live the king!"). Celan comments:

. . . als rings um Camille Pathos und Sentenz den Triumph von "Puppe" und "Draht" bestätigen, da ist Lucile, die Kunstblinde, dieselbe Lucile, für die Sprache etwas Personhaftes und Wahrnehmbares hat, noch einmal da, mit ihrem plötzlichen "Es lebe der König!" Nach allen auf der Tribüne (es ist das Blutgerüst) gesprochenen Worten—welch ein Wort! Es ist das Gegenwort, es ist das Wort, das den "Draht" zerreißt, . . . es ist ein Akt der Freiheit. . . . Gehuldigt wird hier der für die Gegenwart des Menschlichen zeugenden Majestät des Absurden.

(As all around Camille bathos and oratory confirm the triumph of "puppet" and "string," there is Lucile, the one blind to art, the same Lucile for whom language has personal and perceptible [the components of the word mean literally "truth-taking"] qualities, once again there, with her sudden "Long live the king!" After all the words spoken on the platform (the executioners')—what a word! It is the counter-word, it is the word which severs the "string," . . . it is an act of freedom. . . . What is acknowledged here is the majesty of the Absurd, which gives testimony to the presence of mankind.)

Celan previously characterized Lucile as one who can "hear the speaker and 'sees him speak.'" This calls to mind the passage from "Edgar Jené und der Traum vom Traume" in which a mingling of the senses is a prerequisite for a successful

escape from the realm of reason into the state in which true—
irrational—reality can be intuitively comprehended. Celan, the
master of the obscure metaphor, seldom expresses himself so
directly. Lucile "sees" the absurdity of life and of the deaths of
Camille and his companions. She refuses to remain a prisoner of
the revolution and asserts her freedom by screaming out a
"counter-word," a word which does not praise the monarchy
and which is not aimed at the ideals of the revolution, but one
directed against the *tyranny* of the revolution, and the tyranny
of fate over human beings. It is irrational, yet it is the only
adequate expression of her own refusal to be a part of the
historical process and her insistence on maintaining her individual human dignity.

In the speech Celan continues to be torn between the two
possibilities of art (or poetry): the dehumanizing and the
liberating. Before proceeding to a discussion of Büchner's story,
Lenz, he almost casually drops a remark that his stubbornness
in discussing the same subject at such length "liegt wohl in der
Luft—in der Luft, die wir zu atmen haben" ("probably lies in
the air—in the air, which is there for us to breathe"). This is one
of the many direct references in Celan to the composition of the
air we breathe. Since the time of the cremation of millions of
Jews, the air has contained their remains, and the poet connot
forget this.[13] Following this subtle allusion to his own position
as a Jew—and German poet—Celan proceeds to a discussion of
a possible way out of the dilemma—explicitly, the dilemma of art
and poetry, and implicitly the dilemma of his own relation to it:

Finden wir jetzt vielleicht den Ort, . . . wo die Person sich freizusetzen
vermochte, als ein—befremdetes—Ich? . . . ". . . nur war es ihm manchmal unangenehm, daß er nicht auf dem Kopf gehen konnte."—Das ist
er, Lenz. Das ist, glaube ich, er und sein Schritt, er und sein "Es
lebe der König". . . . Wer auf dem Kopf geht, meine Damen und
Herren,—wer auf dem Kopf geht, der hat den Himmel als Abgrund
unter sich.

(Do we now perhaps find the place . . . where a person is able to
set himself free, as an—alienated—individual? . . . "It just bothered
him sometimes that he was not able to walk standing on his head."—
That is he, Lenz. That is, I believe, he and his step, he and his
"Long live the king." . . . Whoever walks standing on his head, ladies

and gentlemen,—whoever walks standing on his head, has heaven underneath himself as an abyss.)

Lenz, by identifying the heavens with the abyss, proclaims the absurdity of life, just as Lucile does with her exclamation. Celan further elaborates: "Lenz—das heißt Büchner—ist hier einen Schritt weiter gegangen als Lucile. Sein 'Es lebe der König' ist kein Wort mehr, es ist ein furchtbares Verstummen, es verschlägt ihm—und auch uns—den Atem und das Wort. Dichtung: das kann eine Atemwende bedeuten." ("Lenz—that is, Büchner— has here gone one step further than Lucile. His 'Long live the king' is no longer a word; it is a terrible falling silent, it takes away his breath and word, and ours, too. Poetry: it can represent a resumption and reorientation of breathing.") The "Atemwende" is a change in direction, a rejection of the path which fate has chosen, in whatever manner is possible. The two examples cited, Lucile and Lenz, imply individual defiance and a reversal of the generally accepted world order, political or transcendental.

At the end of the speech Celan develops a complicated word play based on the Greek *topos*, literally "place," but also a rhetorical term and a component of "Utopia," literally "no place." A few paragraphs later Celan describes his own search for a place:

Ich suche das alles mit wohl sehr ungenauem, weil unruhigem Finger auf der Landkarte—auf einer Kinder-Landkarte, wie ich gleich gestehen muß. Keiner dieser Orte ist zu finden, es gibt sie nicht, aber ich weiß, wo es sie, zumal jetzt, geben müßte, und ... ich finde etwas! ... Ich finde das Verbindende und wie das Gedicht zur Begegnung Führende. Ich finde etwas—wie die Sprache—Immaterielles, aber Irdisches, Terrestrisches, etwas Kreisförmiges, ... — ... ich finde ... einen *Meridian*.

(I search for all that with an unsteady and therefore restless finger on the map—on a child's map, as I must confess right away. None of these places is to be found, they do not exist; but I know where they—at least now—should be, and ... I find something! ... I find that which connects and that which, like the poem, leads to an encounter. I find something—like language—immaterial but earth-bound, terrestrial, something circular, ... I find ... a *meridian*.)

The twelve final lines of the speech consist of seemingly mean-ingless expressions of thanks, and they are even omitted from the text of the speech printed in the *Ausgewählte Gedichte* of 1968. But they are quite significant. Hans Mayer has commented on the great care with which Celan formulated even the message on a postcard to a friend,[14] and with how much more care must he have formulated every word in his only extended public speech, even the apparently routine and insignificant closing remarks: "Ich werde mich daran erinnern dürfen, daß ich neben Menschen, deren Person und deren Werk mir Begegnung bedeuten, Träger eines Preises bin, der Georg Büchners gedenkt. Herzlich danke ich . . . für diesen Augenblick und für diese Begegnung." ("I will be able to remember that I am, along with writers whose person and whose work means an encounter to me, the recipient of a prize in honor of George Büchner. I thank you sincerely . . . for this moment and for this encounter.") These words are followed by a series of expressions of specific thanks, in which the word "danken" is repeated altogether seven times. "Begegnung," it must be noted, is an ambiguous word. It signifies a coming together, but not necessarily a friendly one. And Celan does indeed encounter or "confront" Gottfried Benn here, just as he is confronted by Benn in accepting the prize previously held by that poet. The effusive expression of thanks is ironic. Celan here follows and builds upon the precedent he established in the opening paragraph of the Bremen speech. Another example of excessive—ironic—politeness in *Der Meridian* is the insertion of the phrase "Meine Damen und Herren" ("Ladies and Gentlemen") a total of eighteen times in the printed text. Celan, in his own subtle way, is telling the members of his German audience that they, like Brutus, are honorable men.

The "meridian" also has a personal meaning for the poet. The language in the final passage suggests—and a later poem confirms—that this something, "immaterial" yet "terrestrial," is in fact the Jewish dead, "in the air, which is there for us to breathe." The concluding poem of *Die Niemandsrose* (1963) contains the following lines, which unmistakably establish the relationship between the meridian and the Jewish victims: "In der Luft, da bleibt deine Wurzel, da . . .// Groß/ geht der Verbannte dort oben, der/ Verbrannte . . .// Mit ihm/ wandern die Meridiane." ("In the air, there your root remains, there. . . . Large, the exiled one goes up there, the burned one. . . . With him the meridians wander," NR, 88). Somehow the poet develops a sense of identity with the Jewish dead. His own life, as a person and as a poet writing in German, acquires meaning through them and through his awareness of their continuing presence in the air around him.

IV "Gespräch im Gebirg"

Celan's only piece of "prose fiction" is entitled "Gespräch im Gebirg" ("Dialogue in the Mountains"). This highly poetic text, which was written in August, 1959, can readily be identified as representing a very early stage in the poet's restoration of his relationship to Judaism. The autobiographical nature of the story is confirmed in the Meridian speech, where Celan, specifically referring to it says: "Ich bin ... mir selbst begegnet" ("I ... encountered myself," Mer, 86). The beginning of the story describes the encounter:

Eines Abends, die Sonne, und nicht nur sie, war untergegangen, da ging, trat aus seinem Häusel und ging der Jud, der Jud und Sohn eines Juden.... ging, wie Lenz, durchs Gebirg.... Entgegen kam ihm sein Vetter, sein Vetter und Geschwisterkind, der um ein Viertel Judenleben älter, groß kam er daher, kam, auch er, in dem Schatten, dem geborgten—denn welcher, so frag und frag ich, kommt, da Gott ihn hat einen Juden sein lassen, daher mit Eignem?—, kam, kam groß, kam dem andern entgegen, Groß kam auf Klein zu.[15]

(One evening, the sun had gone down and not it alone, the Jew left his little house and went, the Jew and son of a Jew ... went like Lenz through the mountains.... Towards him came his kinsman and cousin, who was a quarter of a Jewish life older, large, he came from the opposite direction, he too, came, in the shadow, which was borrowed—for who, I ask and ask, comes, if God has made him a Jew, comes with his own?—Large approached Small.)

The reference to a quarter of a Jewish life would seem to suggest the fifteen years between the end of the war and the composition of the story. Celan here meets himself, the self of the period immediately following the war. The older Jew's name, Gross (Large), develops from an allusion (the first of several) to "Edgar Jené und der Traum vom Traume," in which "Der Sohn des Nordlichts ... kommt groß vorüber" (literally: "large, passes by"). The Celan of 1948, who had decided to turn away from Judaism, now returns, meets his younger cousin—the more recent self of 1959—and a conversation develops. The individual speakers are not immediately identified. Only in the final speech is it made clear that the words belong to Klein (Little), the Celan of 1959. Then the identity of the speaker of each of the preceding statements can be ascertained.

Gross expresses pessimistic thoughts early in the dialogue: "Es hat sich die Erde gefaltet hier oben, hat sich gefaltet einmal und zweimal und dreimal. . . . Das Weiße kommt von noch weiter oben, kommt von den Gletschern" ("The earth folded itself up here, folded itself twice and three times. . . . The whiteness comes from still farther up there, comes from the glaciers"). Here Celan puns on a German word for the Trinity, "Dreifaltigkeit" (literally: "three-fold-ness"), when he says that the earth folded itself three times. The allusion to the northerly glaciers, also reminiscent of "Der Sohn des Nordlichts," reflects the extremely negative conception of God held by the Jew Gross. He goes on, in the process of establishing the cold, godless, impersonal nature of the landscape, to refer to language, "eine Sprache . . . ohne Ich und ohne Du" ("A language . . . without I and without thou"). Klein then takes up the reference to God: "Hörstdu, der sagt nichts, der antwortet nicht, denn Hörstdu, das ist der mit den Gletschern, der, der sich gefaltet hat, dreimal, und nicht für die Menschen." ("Do-you-hear, he says nothing, he doesn't answer, for Do-you-hear, that is the one with the glaciers, he, who folded himself, three times, and not for mankind.") As Peter Mayer has observed, Celan here alludes to Deuteronomy 6:4ff., "Hear, Israel, the Eternal, our God, the Eternal is one Lord [einzig]," and probably to Hermann Cohen's interpretation of this passage as an indication of "the Judaic conception of unity."[16] If such a reference is present—and this would seem highly likely—it has decidedly ironic overtones. The "unity" of the Jewish God has just been denied in the rather irreverent allusion to the Christian Trinity; Cohen's rationalistic, optimistic interpretation, Celan implies, has been refuted by history. God, "Höre, Israel," "Hörstdu," has folded himself three times, and no good for mankind has resulted.

Klein continues, saying that he lay on the stone floor near, but separated from, the "other cousins," who "schliefen und schliefen nicht, . . . träumten und träumten nicht" ("slept and did not sleep, dreamed and did not dream")—another reference to the Jené essay. He further elaborates on their relationship:

Ich liebte sie nicht, sie, die mich nicht lieben konnten, ich liebte die Kerze, die da brannte, links im Winkel, ich liebte sie, weil sie herunter-brannte, nicht weil *sie* herunterbrannte, denn *sie,* das war ja *seine* Kerze, die Kerze, die er, der Vater unsrer Mütter, angezündet hatte, weil an jenem Abend ein Tag begann, ein bestimmter, ein Tag, der der siebte war, der siebte, auf den der erste folgen sollte, der siebte und nicht der letzte, ich liebte, Geschwisterkind, nicht sie, ich liebte ihr Herunterbrennen, und weißt du, ich habe nichts mehr geliebt seither.

(I didn't love them, they, who could not love me, I loved the candle, which burned there, in the corner at the left, I loved it because it burned down, not because *it* burned down, for *it,* after all, was *his* candle, the candle which he, the father of our mothers, had lighted, because on that evening a day began, a specific day, which was the seventh, the seventh, upon which the first was to follow, the seventh and not the last, I loved, cousin, not it, I loved its burning-down and, you know, I have loved nothing else since that time.)

The reference is to the Sabbath candle, which is traditionally lighted prior to the official beginning of the Sabbath. A woman always lights the candle, unless there is no woman living in the household. Friday evening is a happy time of family together-ness during which the candle burns down slowly. In the story the candle is lighted by the father. This suggests that God the Father lights the candle for Israel (alluding to the creation of light in Genesis), but also refers to the absence of Celan's own dead mother. The candle is God's, and hence the speaker can-not love it. But he does now love its burning, which is reminiscent of his former personal happiness and his present affection for the Jewish dead. The emotional implications of the Sabbath candle can be seen in the concluding remarks of Jakob Soetendorp as he describes the Sabbath ritual in his book *Symbolik der jüdi-schen Religion*: "... The family celebrates being together. Must I emphasize that I am able to write these lines only with diffi-culty? The Jewish communities have become small, and they have almost vanished in much of Europe. ...They [the rituals of the Sabbath evening] remain merely a touching memory for those few [still living] who were able to experience them."[17]

The final lines of the story, still spoken by Klein, return to the poet's personal interpretation of his Jewish past and present:

... die Falten dort, du weißt, nicht für die Menschen sind sie da und nicht für uns, die wir gingen und einander trafen, wir hier unterm Stern, wir, die Juden, die da kamen .... Ich mit der herunter-gebrannten, der Kerze, ich mit dem Tag, ich mit den Tagen, ich hier und ich dort, ich, begleitet vielleicht—jetzt!—von der Liebe der Nichtgeliebten, ich auf dem Wege hier zu mir, oben.

(The folds there, you know, they are not there for mankind and not for us, we who went and encountered each other, we here under the star, we, the Jews, who came .... I with the candle which burned down, I with the day, I with the days, I here and I there, I, accompanied, perhaps—now!—by the love of those who were not loved, I on the road here to myself, above.)

The folds—the Trinity—are not for men and not for us, for us Jews. On one level Celan is saying that he, Gross and Klein, is set apart from other men. He is also alluding to the Nazi dis-tinction between human beings and Jews—who were treated like animals—a concept which regularly appears in the poetry. Now Celan returns to Judaism, having been isolated from it, in some respects, for a period of time. The change in attitude reflects the difference between the poems of *Sprachgitter* (1959) and *Die Niemandsrose* (1963), which will be discussed in Chapters 5 and 6, respectively.

CHAPTER 3

Early Poems and Mohn und Gedächtnis

I The Early Poems

THE first important collection of Celan's poems, seventeen in all, was published in 1948 in Otto Basil's periodical *Plan*. Fifteen of these were included in *Der Sand aus den Urnen* (*The Sand from the Urns*), which appeared later that same year. This book was recalled almost immediately by the author and very few copies were actually sold. One reason for the recall of the book, and the one invariably cited, is the presence of several typographical errors. Celan was very particular about such matters, and when he discovered the misprints he was greatly disturbed. He also expressed dissatisfaction with the appearance of the cover of the book. The cover was not especially attractive, but one could hardly have expected it to be otherwise, considering the economic conditions prevalent in Vienna at the time. Another reason for the recall was probably the poet's growing dissatisfaction with many of his early poems, a dissatisfaction which becomes intelligible when the contents of *Mohn und Gedächtnis* (*Poppy and Memory*, 1952) are compared with those of the *Plan* collection and with *Der Sand aus den Urnen*. Of the seventeen poems included in *Plan*, two were omitted from *Der Sand aus der Urnen*, which appeared only a few months later. Furthermore, all seventeen poems of the first cycle of *Der Sand aus den Urnen*, as well as four poems from the latter part of the book, are omitted from *Mohn und Gedächtnis*.

Many of these early poems are written in rhyme and most are —at least at first glance—rather romantic. More significantly, perhaps, several of them are intensely personal, especially "Nähe der Gräber" ("Nearness of Graves," SU, 14) and "Schwarze Flocken" ("Black Flakes," SU, 19). The former poem consists of five rhymed couplets, each of which is a question addressed

47

to the poet's dead mother. The final couplet is especially poignant:

> Und duldest du, Mutter, wie einst, ach, daheim,
> den leisen, den deutschen, den schmerzlichen Reim?

(And can you still bear, mother, as formerly, alas, at home, the soft, the German, the painful rhyme?)

These lines offer a rare insight into Celan's mind. It was obviously difficult for him to continue to write poetry in German, yet he felt compelled to do so. Critics have noted the paradox that Celan was forced to write in the language of the Nazis, but have not sufficiently emphasized its importance. As a parallel case Jakov Lind (born 1927) can be cited. In a speech delivered at Hebrew Union College, Cincinnati, Ohio, in April, 1966, Lind said: "The only language I have is German, and I hear it from the mouth of the oppressor." Elie Wiesel relates an anecdote which illustrates his attitude toward the German language. He reports that during his only postwar trip to Germany he was walking alone on a street when "a young woman came up and asked me the way to the station. I told her I did not know, that I was a stranger. She smiled. I almost smiled back, when my lips suddenly froze: I became aware that I had been speaking German."[1] The lines from "Nähe der Gräber" demonstrate that Celan was in fact intimately aware of the dilemma, and especially of the implications of the German rhyme, since rhyme, as a poetic device, specifically draws the attention of the reader to the language itself. This is one of the reasons why rhyme is used sparingly in his poetry, and it is for this reason also that the places in which it is used tend to be, at least in all but the earliest poetry, quite intense and bitter.

Small but significant changes were made in the poem "Schwarze Flocken" for publication in *Der Sand aus den Urnen*. The first three lines of the final version of the poem run: "Schnee ist gefallen, lichtlos. Ein Mond/ ist es schon oder zwei, daß der Herbst unter mönchischer Kutte/ Botschaft brachte auch mir, ein Blatt aus ukrainischen Halden" ("Snow has fallen, lightless. One moon or two has it been since autumn in the garb of a monk brought a message also to me, a leaf from Ukrainian slopes"). The first two lines, as originally printed in *Plan*, are: "Schnee ist

gefallen, lichtlos. Ein Mond/ ach kaum oder zwei ist es her, daß
der Herbst unter mönchischer Kutte..." ("Snow has fallen,
lightless. Scarcely one moon, alas, or two, has it been since
autumn, in the garb of a monk...""). The degree of intimacy is
reduced, and the objectivity slightly enhanced in the second version, indicating that the poet is already beginning to move away
from the intimate, personal mode of expression characteristic
of many very early poems. The title of the version printed in
Plan is "Schnee ist gefallen," a formulation that is more romantic
than the sinister "Schwarze Flocken."

The second section of the poem, in both versions, consists of
twelve lines, set apart by quotation marks, which constitute
the mother's "letter."[2] A few lines will illustrate the intensely
personal nature of this passage: "... Kind, ach ein Tuch,/ mich zu
hüllen darein, wenn es blinket von Helmen,/ wenn die Scholle,
die rosige, birst, wenn schneeig stäubt das Gebein/ deines
Vaters" ("Child, alas, a cloth to cover me with, when the helmets
glisten, when the earth, the rosy one, bursts, when snow-like
the bones of your father turn to dust"). This is the only reference to his own father to be found in all of Celan's poetry, and
it is quite significant that it appears in the form of a quotation,
in words spoken by the mother. It is not unlikely that the guilt
from which Celan suffered his entire life was in some way linked
to the relationship between his parents and himself, and, perhaps,
to the mother's unsuccessful attempt to reconcile the father and
the son while all three were still alive. Following the quotation,
the poem continues: "Blutete, Mutter, der Herbst mir hinweg,
brannte der Schnee mich" ("When the autumn bled away,
mother, the snow burned me"). It is apparent from this poem
that "Schnee" "Blatt," and, especially, "Herbst" are ciphers—
private symbols—in Celan's poetry. Autumn is, for him, the time
of the year when his mother was killed, or when he learned of
her death; and, accordingly, when the stamp of finality is placed
upon his relationship to his parents and his past. Snow and leaves
are reminders of this time.

Although the remaining fifteen poems contained in this cycle,
"An den Toren" ("At the Gates"), are not as intimate, the
seventeen together form a unit and the few intensely personal
passages lend an emotional cast to the other poems. The very
structure of the cycle contains an implicit statement of Celan's

attitude toward the Jewish religion or God. It is significant
that there are seventeen poems in the collection. The penultimate
poem, "Die Schwelle des Traumes" ("The Threshhold of
Dream," SU, 20), contains the lines: "Es war meine Seele ihr
Sieb, gefüllt sind nun siebzehn Krüge/ ... Ich geh noch vors
Haus zu forschen nach Wasser im Sande:/ leer blieb der letzte,
der achtzehnte Krug" ("My soul was the sieve, seventeen jugs are
now filled ... I step out of the house to search for water in the
sand: the final, the eighteenth jug remained empty"). Here, as
often in Celan's poetry, water represents a saving or potentially
saving element. But the last jug remains empty; the promise of
the water remains unfulfilled. The next poem, the seventeenth
and last of the cycle, is entitled "Am letzten Tor" ("At the Last
Gate," SU, 21). The first line contains the word "Herbst,"
thereby establishing the emotional tone of the poem and suggesting a sense of loss: "Herbst hab ich in Gottes Herz ge-
sponnen" ("I have spun autumn in God's heart").

The numbers seventeen and eighteen refer to the Jewish
"Eighteen-Prayer." The breaking off of the cycle after seventeen
poems, as well as the emptiness of the eighteenth jug, indicate
that the speaker no longer wishes to recite the prayer to the end
(and not, as it might seem, that he has forgotten the prayer).
The opening and closing lines of the eighteenth and final section
of the prayer are: "Spread your peace over Israel, your people.
... Praise be to you, Lord, who provides peace."[3] God has not
brought peace to Israel, and the speaker accordingly refuses to
praise God by reciting the prayer. A "Widerruf" of an affirmative
Hassidic tale is also present here. After Rabbi Mendel's wife and
daughter die, Buber relates, the holy man prays the Eighteen-
Prayer and then reaffirms his faith. "Now I have no one except
you [God] to bring joy to my life. Thus I will rejoice in you."[4]
Whereas the tale reaffirms the man's faith in spite of the loss of
his family, Celan cannot praise God under the circumstances, and
he denies the literal religious aspects of the Jewish heritage.
The "Herbst" motif, developed so clearly in the poem "Schwarze
Flocken," appears once again in the final poem of the cycle.
Autumn was the time of the year when the "Blatt" came from
the mother, and the falling of leaves is also alluded to in "Am
letzten Tor": "Wie das Laub verstreuet, ist vertan der Wein"
("Just as the foliage is scattered, so the wine is wasted").

The connotations of autumn and the falling or fallen leaf continue to appear in Celan's poetry and invariably evoke associations similar to those encountered in the early poems under discussion. Celan was in Paris at the time of the appearance of *Der Sand aus den Urnen.* He had already begun his new life, and a desire to sever certain ties with his past undoubtedly was a major factor in his decision to recall his first collection of poems.

II Mohn und Gedächtnis: "Der Sand aus den Urnen"

The cyclical principle of *Der Sand aus den Urnen* is continued in *Mohn und Gedächtnis.* The book is divided into four sections: "Der Sand aus den Urnen" (twenty-five poems); "Todesfuge"; "Gegenlicht" ("Counter-light," seventeen poems); and "Halme der Nacht" ("Blades of Night," thirteen poems). As Siegbert Prawer has observed, the somber mood of the collection is established in the first poem, "Ein Lied in der Wüste" ("A Song in the Desert," MG, 7).[5] The ominous tone is present from the very first line: "Ein Kranz ward gewunden aus schwärzlichem Laub in der Gegend von Akra" ("A wreath was formed out of blackish foliage in the vicinity of Akra"). The poem at first puzzled critics, which is not surprising since many of its images are extremely difficult to fathom and seem to lack any specific frame of reference. Early interpreters of the poem often dismissed the images as "surrealistic," implying that they existed for their own sake and lacked any connection with a systematic pattern of thought and emotion. But recent critics have identified the frame of reference of many of the images, and this poem, as well as others in the collection, can, accordingly, be interpreted in a meaningful manner.

Two religious references in "Ein Lied in der Wüste" have been identified by Peter Mayer, and these would seem to offer the most fruitful basis for interpretation.[6] Mayer perceptively observes that two lines, "Denn tot sind die Engel und blind ward der Herr in der Gegend von Akra,/ ... Zuschanden gehaun ward der Mond, das Blümlein der Gegend von Akra" ("For the angels are dead, and the Lord turned blind in the vicinity of Akra ... the moon, the little flower of the vicinity of Akra, was chopped to pieces"), constitute the reversal of a Biblical passage: "The sun shall be no more thy light by day; neither for brightness shall the moon give light unto thee: but the Lord shall be unto thee an everlasting light, and thy God thy glory. Thy sun shall no more go down; neither shall thy moon withdraw itself: for the Lord shall be thine everlasting light, . . . and the days of thy mourning shall be ended" (Isa. 60: 19f.). The second religious reference occurs in the line "So ward ich ihr lächelnder Bruder, der eiserne Cherub von Akra" ("So I became its smiling brother, the iron cherub of Akra"). On this line Mayer comments: "It was the 'iron cherub,' as distinguished from the golden cherub in the temple." The poem, then, contains a refutation of a Biblical passage which promises the end of the sufferings of the Jewish people, as well as a specific example of the transformation of a positive religious image (the golden cherub of the temple) into a negative one (the iron cherub of Akra).

Once this frame of reference is established, the significance of the name "Akra" becomes apparent. The word, which means "a fortress," is the specific name of a geographical region in Jerusalem, apparently located directly south of the temple. It was the site of battles significant for the Jewish people, both at the time of the fall of Jerusalem to Titus in A.D. 70, and at the time of the Maccabees, as the historian Josephus reports.[7] The poem, then, consists of a series of surrealistic images which, upon closer examination, are seen to refer to early battles in which the Jewish people were engaged, including the one which resulted in the destruction of Jerusalem by the Romans, which Jesus is said to have predicted when he said: "Daughters of Jerusalem, weep not for me, but weep for yourselves, and for your children" (Luke 23:28). The poem also introduces the traditional ancient symbol of the rose as an image of the Jewish people. But Celan changes the image: "so blühn, die den Dornen es gleichtun, die Hände mit rostigen Ringen" ("In this manner bloom those which are similar to the thorns, the hands with rusty rings"). The ring is a symbol of fidelity, and the rustiness here suggests a disintegration, referring to God's broken pledges to his chosen people and to the resulting alienation between God and the speaker.

If the first poem of the cycle establishes the general tone of Jewish defeats in the past and calls to mind the failure of the Lord to keep his promise—"Your sorrow will end"—the poems which immediately follow are more personal. Each of the next five poems contains some form of the word "Blatt," which, as was note above, is a cipher in Celan's poetry associated with the death of the mother. The first eight poems of the cycle are difficult and contain many surrealistic elements. They abound in negative images and references: the grave, suffering, daggers, death. Several images which will recur in the poetry are introduced, such as water and hair, but their specific implications, like the meanings of most of the poems, are not immediately apparent. The ninth poem, "Espenbaum" ("Aspen Tree," MG, 15), marks a distinct change in atmosphere. The poem consists of five couplets, like "Nähe der Gräber," but is unrhymed. The first line of each couplet is an observation, apparently without negative implications, relating to an object in nature; but the second line invariably contains a specific reference to the mother. Each pair of lines indicates how the speaker perceives individual aspects of nature in terms of the dead mother. For example, in one couplet the sight of the white foliage of the aspen tree, which can be seen through the darkness, reminds him of his mother's hair, which never became gray because she died at an early age in the concentration camp:

> Espenbaum, dein Laub blickt weiß ins Dunkel.
> Meiner Mutter Haar ward nimmer weiß.

(Aspen tree, your foliage gazes white into the darkness. My mother's hair never turned white.)

The third stanza introduces water imagery, especially the image of the well, again establishing an association with the mother, in this case with her tears:

> Regenwolke, säumst du an den Brunnen?
> Meine leise Mutter weint für alle.

(Rain cloud, do you tarry by the well? Gentle, my mother cries for all.)

The remaining poems of the cycle are, for the most part, difficult and continue in the style of the first portion of the collection; they contain long lines, many genitive metaphors (such as "in den Spiegeln des Todes" ["in the mirrors of death"], and "Die Sonnen des Todes" ["the suns of death"], etc.), and numerous repetitions of key images, especially hair, autumn, weapons, and water in various forms.

The penultimate poem of the cycle "Spät und tief" ("Late and Deep," MG, 31f.), like its first poem, contains a definite reference to an event in the early history of the Jewish people. A few lines from this difficult poem will establish the tone as well as the frame of reference:

Wir schwören bei Christus dem Neuen, den Staub zu vermählen dem Staube,/ . . . Wir schwören der Welt die heiligen Schwüre des Sandes,// . . . Sie rufen: Ihr lästert!// . . . Ihr mahnt uns: Ihr lästert!/ Wir wissen es wohl,/es komme die Schuld über uns./ . . . es komme/ . . . der mitternächtige Tag,/es komme was niemals noch war!//Es komme ein Mensch aus dem Grabe.

(We swear by Christ, the New, to wed dust to dust. . . . We swear to the world the holy vows of the sand . . . they call out: you blaspheme. You admonish us: you blaspheme! We know; let guilt be upon us, let the midnight-day come, let there come what never has been! Let a man come out of the grave.)

The poem is an extented reference to, and commentary upon, the Biblical passage describing the trial of Jesus, within which the Jews accept the responsibility for his death and ask that his blood be on them and on their children (Matt. 27:25). This is, of course, one Biblical passage upon which Christian anti-Semitism is based. The "midnight day" is a reference to the blackness at the time of the crucifixion. The parallel grammatical forms at the end of the poem, "es komme die Schuld, . . . es komme ein Mensch," express the speakers' denial of the possibility of the Resurrection, and of the validity of the Christian assignment of guilt to the Jews. The first cycle concludes with the poem "Corona" ("Crown," or "Wreath," MG, 33), which, as will be shown below, refers to the "wreath" of time, the circular, repetitive nature of the events of which the modern persecution of the Jewish people consists. The poem closes with a plea for a change, "it is time" for the persecutions to cease.

III Mohn und Gedächtnis: "Gegenlicht" and "Halme der Nacht"

The second section of the book consists of but a single poem, "Todesfuge" (MG, 37-39), Celan's most famous and impressive work, which will be analyzed at length below. "Todesfuge" immediately follows "Corona" and vividly depicts the Nazi death

camps, thereby illustrating why it is high time for a change to
be made. The title "Gegenlicht" ("Counter-Light") and the
first poem of the next section indicate that the cyclical principle
is still in force.[8] "Gegenlicht" implies that a person is facing
a light which comes from the opposite direction, but it could
also refer to the light itself, which is directed against something
or someone. The word is used in "Edgar Jené und der Traum
vom Traume," where it is associated with death: "Oft haben
wir als Wache geschworen: im heißen Schatten ungeduldiger
Fahnen, im Gegenlicht des fremden Todes, am Hochaltar
unserer heiliggesprochenen Vernunft" ("We often swore as
sentinels [or: while awake]: in the hot shadow of impatient
banners, in the counter-light of the alien death, on the high altar
of our canonized rationality"). The significance of the word in
the two contexts seems to be slightly different. In the essay the
speaker stands in the opposing light of Judaic culture, implying
a force countering the light of the gospel of St. John. Now
Celan, or his poetry, is the counter-light; he is changing his
direction, opposing the past.

The first poem of the cycle, "Auf Reisen" ("Traveling," MG,
43), confirms the interpretation that Celan is moving away from
at least some aspects of his past. This poem was included in
Der Sand aus den Urnen, where it preceded "Todesfuge," and
must accordingly have been written in Vienna, before Celan
moved to Paris. Yet it contains the words "dein Haus in Paris"
("your house in Paris"). The position of the poem, with its
reference to the poet's new home, at the beginning of the cycle
and following "Todesfuge," reinforces the idea of a turning
away from the past. The poet moves to France, away from the
German language and other aspects of his heritage; "Auf Reisen,"
too, now points forward.

The second poem of the cycle, "In Ägypten" ("In Egypt"),
likewise suggests that the relationship of the speaker to his
Jewish past may be changing. The poem mentions an "alien
woman" in conjunction with three Jewish names: "Du sollst zu
Ruth und Mirjam und Noëmi sagen:/ Seht, ich schlaf bei ihr!/
... Du sollst zur Fremden sagen:/ Sieh, ich schlief bei diesen!"
("Say to Ruth and Mirjam and Noemi, see, I sleep with her!
Say to the alien woman, see, I slept with them!"). The speaker
is with an alien woman, a Gentile. On one level, this is an actual

person, a lover, and on another level the stranger is his new, non-Jewish way of life. He must remind his new lover that he has previously slept with the Jewish women, or remind his new French neighbors that he is Jewish and that he has emotional ties to his tradition. But, at the same time, he insists that a break has taken place: he tells the Jewish women that he is now attached to the alien.

In many of the poems of "Gegenlicht" and "Halme der Nacht" ("Blades of Night"), the fourth and final section of the book, indications of a change in style are evident. The long lines and dactylic rhythm generally characteristic of the poems of the first two sections become less prominent. To be sure, the images, for the most part, remain constant; such lines as "Wer sein Herz aus der Brust reißt zur Nacht, der langt nach der Rose" ("Whoever tears his heart out of his breast at night reaches for the rose," MG, 49), or "Der Hauch der Nacht ist dein Laken, die Finsternis legt sich zu dir" ("The breath of night is your sheet, darkness lies down with you," MG, 63) are quite similar to typical lines from the earlier poems. But several innovations may also be seen. On the one hand, more of the poems seem, on the surface, to be love poems—such as "In Ägypten"—and on the other hand an increasing preoccupation with the poetic "word" is evident. Celan seems to be struggling to free himself from his past by turning his attention to love and poetry.

The Jewish and personal elements are by no means absent, however. The rose is mentioned repeatedly, often in conjunction with the thorn, suggesting Israel and her sufferings or enemies: "Stille! Der Dorn dringt dir tiefer ins Herz:/ Er steht im Bund mit der Rose." ("Still! the thorn bores deeper into your heart. It is allied with the rose," MG, 73). The final poem of the collection, "Zähle die Mandeln" ("Count the Almonds," MG, 76), clearly indicates the poet's continuing concern with the past. Several complicated allusions are contained in the first stanza:

> Zähle die Mandeln,
> zähle, was bitter war und dich wachhielt,
> zähl mich dazu:

(Count the almonds, count that which was bitter and kept you awake, count me among them:)

The original association of counting with "Mandeln" is based upon an archaic meaning of the word; in addition to "almond," it is a measuring unit of fifteen or sixteen items. The word also becomes in Celan a cipher for the Jews, particularly because of an association with the name of Osip Mandelshtam, a Russian Jew and poet who died during the Stalinist purges of the 1930's. A further word play is at work in the second line, based upon the similarity of the Hebrew words for "almond" and "awake," as exploited in Jeremiah, 1:11-13. The essay "Edgar Jené und der Traum vom Traume" is also called to mind. In that essay Celan says: "Oft haben wir als Wache geschworen.... Laßt uns also versuchen, im Schlafe zu schwören" ("We have often sworn while awake [or: as sentinels].... So let us try to swear in sleep"). Being awake is a negative condition in Celan, related to— but by no means identical with—the painful condition of memory. "Bitter" here refers to the taste of the almonds and also to an important Hassidic parable related as follows by Buber: "When a man suffers he should not say 'it is bad, it is bad.' Nothing that God does to man is bad. But one may say 'it is bitter,' for there are bitter drugs among the medicinal remedies."[9] As often, Buber's affirmative Hassidism is denied by Celan. In "Zähle die Mandeln," the speaker is asking to be numbered among the Jews, so many of whom are dead. The allusion to Buber's parable, with its reference to the goodness of God, elicits the ironic use of the word "bitter."

A poem which underscores the speaker's inability to free himself from his past is "Der Reisekamerad" ("The Travel Companion," MG, 64). The title alludes to "Auf Reisen," the first poem of "Gegenlicht." The companion who is accompanying the speaker on his journey away from the past, as the poem explicitly states, is none other than the mother's soul. In the second of the two short stanzas, the relationship between the mother and the speaker's attempt to write in a new and foreign environment is explained:

> Dieses Wort ist deiner Mutter Mündel.
> Deiner Mutter Mündel teilt dein Lager, Stein um Stein.
> Deiner Mutter Mündel bückt sich nach der Krume Lichts.

(This word is your mother's ward. Your mother's ward shares your campsite [or: bed] stone for stone. Your mother's ward bends down for the crumb of light.)

The speaker's words remain the "ward" of the dead mother, that is, the memory of the mother still exerts a strong control over the poems. The poems, in turn, share the "camp" of the poet; he must write, he cannot free himself from either this compulsion or from the past. The vocabulary—camp, crumb, and, indirectly, stone—is suggestive of the concentration camps.

Another poem which deals with the same problem is "So bist du denn geworden" ("And this is what you have become," MG, 57). In a highly unusual oral statement Celan has confirmed that this poem is addressed to his mother.[10] The concluding lines of the poem, following ten lines which describe the presence of a thou (the mother) in a watery landscape, are: "Du hast ein Spiel ersonnen,/ das will vergessen sein." ("You have thought of a game, which ought to be forgotten"). As in the poem "Der Reisekamerad," the speaker is bound to the memory of the mother. Here, however, he makes explicit the feeling which is so often implicitly present in the poems: a desire to forget. The title of the collection, *Mohn und Gedächtnis* (*Poppy and Memory*), alludes to this important theme which is especially strong in the poems of the final cycle of the book. The poem "So bist du denn geworden" indicates that the speaker is making progress in his quest for forgetfulness. The tone of the poem is not bitter; it has a remote quality, and the specifically Jewish nature of the death, so often suggested in Celan's earlier poetry, is completely absent.

Several aspects of the theme of memory must be mentioned. First, there is, traditionally, a fundamental difference in attitude between Jews and non-Jews. The following statement by Hermann Hakel makes the distinction quite clear and, in addition, suggests certain ramifications applicable to Celan's specific case:

Jews must have a conscience, not because they are especially noble, but because consciousness produces a conscience and a Jew must never forget that he is a Jew. So his consciousness is overly developed —see Freud. The non-Jew, on the other hand, lives from forgetfulness. It is simply a different relationship to the world.

Many victims of the Nazis have discussed their inability, or even their unwillingness, to forget. Hakel, for example, who lived in Israel for two years after the war, offers the following explanation of his return to Europe: "When people in Israel asked me why I didn't remain there, why I went back to Germany, I responded: 'So that I won't forget what Nazis are.' I will never forget."

Celan seems to attempt to move in the opposite direction; he searches for a different means of coming to terms with the past. He neither goes to Israel nor remains in a German-speaking environment, but moves to a foreign country. There he marries a French gentile who speaks practically no German and has no interest in German literature. He begins to change his style of writing; both the form and the images show signs of a new direction, which will be strikingly confirmed in the next collection, *Von Schwelle zu Schwelle* (*From Threshold to Threshold*, 1955). But the concern with the past is still apparent, both with regard to his Jewishness, as "Zähle die Mandeln" indicates, and specifically with regard to his mother, as "So bist du denn geworden" and "Der Reisekamerad" clearly demonstrate. The break is thus by no means complete.

Many readers today find the poems of *Mohn und Gedächtnis* and, to an even greater extent, of *Der Sand aus den Urnen*, to be old-fashioned and hence unappealing. Certainly the vocabulary is in no sense "modern," and the style—especially on account of the long dactylic lines and frequent genitive metaphors—is likewise reminiscent of a bygone era. But it would be wrong to deny that many of these early poems, which in the 1940's attracted the attention of sensitive critics, remain impressive examples of Celan's poetic talent. If they are viewed as personal and avowedly irrational statements relating to Celan's personal tragedy, the impact of at least some of them is undiminished even today.

IV "Corona"

I have selected two poems for detailed analysis, "Corona" and "Todesfuge." These poems contain numerous allusions to theological and literary sources as well as to Jewish history. Some of these allusions are quite clear whereas others are much less obvious. But they are all functional and contribute to the effect of the poem, and hence must be discussed. It is, of course,

quite possible that the poems contain allusions not referred to
in my interpretation. On one level, "Corona" ("Crown," "Wreath,"
MG, 32) is a "Widerruf" of the poem "Herbsttag" ("Autumn
Day") by Rainer Maria Rilke (1875-1926).[11]

"Herbsttag"

Herr: es ist Zeit. Der Sommer war sehr groß.
Leg deinen Schatten auf die Sonnenuhren,
und auf den Fluren laß die Winde los.

Befiehl den letzten Früchten voll zu sein;
gieb ihnen noch zwei südlichere Tage,
dränge sie zur Vollendung hin und jage
die letzte Süße in den schweren Wein.

Wer jetzt kein Haus hat, baut sich keines mehr.
Wer jetzt allein ist, wird es lange bleiben,
wird wachen, lesen, lange Briefe schreiben
und wird in den Alleen hin und her
unruhig wandern, wenn die Blätter treiben.

(Lord, it is time. The summer was very great. Lay your shadows
on the sundials and release the winds upon the fields.// Command
the last fruits to be ripe; give them two more southerly days, force
them towards fulfillment and drive the last sweetness into the heavy
wine.// Whoever has no house now will not be able to build one.
Whoever is now alone will remain so for a long time, will be awake,
read, write long letters and will wander restlessly in the streets, to
and fro, when the leaves are scattered.)

"Corona"

Aus der Hand frißt der Herbst mir sein Blatt: wir sind Freunde.
Wir schälen die Zeit aus den Nüssen und lehren sie gehn:
die Zeit kehrt zurück in die Schale.

Im Spiegel ist Sonntag,
im Traum wird geschlafen,
der Mund redet wahr.

Mein Aug steigt hinab zum Geschlecht der Geliebten:
wir sehen uns an,
wir sagen uns Dunkles,
wir lieben einander wie Mohn und Gedächtnis,

wir schlafen wie Wein in den Muscheln,
wie das Meer im Blutstrahl des Mondes.

Wir stehen umschlungen im Fenster, sie sehen uns zu von
        der Straße:
es ist Zeit, daß man weiß!
Es ist Zeit, daß der Stein sich zu blühen bequemt,
daß der Unrast ein Herz schlägt.
Es ist Zeit, daß es Zeit wird.

Es ist Zeit.

(Autumn eats its leaf out of my hand: we are friends. We shell
time from the nuts and teach it to walk: time returns to the shells.//
In the mirror there is Sunday, in the dream there is sleeping, the
mouth speaks the truth.// My eye descends to the sex of the beloved
woman [or: to the race of the beloved people]: we look at each
other, we say dark things to each other, we love each other like
poppy and memory, we sleep like wine in the sea shells, like the
sea in the jet of blood of the moon.//We stand in the window,
embracing; they watch us from the street: it is time for people to
know! It is time that the stone condescended to bloom, that a heart
beat for unrest, that it became time.//It is time.)

A number of superficial verbal parallels can be seen between
the two poems. The first line of "Corona" alludes to the title
and the final line of "Herbsttag." Part of Rilke's famous phrase
"Herr: es ist Zeit" is repeated four times toward the end of
Celan's poem; the omission, it should be noted, consists of the
word "Herr," "Lord." There are several components of the
"Widerruf." Basically, Celan turns Rilke's resignation into a
positive assertion, and the absence of the word "Lord" in
Celan's formulation implies a rejection of the acceptance of
God's will which is implicit in Rilke's phrase. The speaker of
"Herbsttag" sees that a period of restlessness and loneliness is
approaching and is prepared to accept this condition. The
speaker of "Corona," on the other hand, cannot say "Lord, thy
will be done." He does not accept as the will of God the fact
that autumn is inevitably coming, autumn with both its traditional values of loneliness, barrenness, and death, and its specific significance for Celan. He not only refuses to accept the
apparently natural phenomenon that the trees will soon be leaf-

less and barren, but he demands a complete reversal of nature:
now even the stones must begin to bloom.

As is usually the case, Biblical and related religious imagery
and references form an integral part of the "Widerruf." A primary
Biblical allusion is to Psalm 102:

Hear my prayer, O Lord, . . . For my days are consumed like smoke,
and my bones are burned as an hearth. . . . Thou shalt arise, and
have mercy upon Zion: for the time to favour her, yea, the set time,
is come [es ist Zeit] . . . This shall be written for the generation to
come: and the people which shall be created shall praise the Lord.

The Lord has not heard the prayer of the Jewish people; they
have, indeed, gone up in smoke. It was time when the Psalms
were composed, and now it is most assuredly time. But the
speaker, a member of the "generation to come," no longer will
praise the Lord. The reason for this change in attitude is indicated by the position of "Corona" in the collection. As many
critics have noted, the poem occupies a key position at the
close of the cycle "Der Sand aus den Urnen"—a phrase suggesting the dust of the Jewish victims—and immediately before
"Todesfuge." The Lord has not "had mercy on Zion"; the references to the dust of the dead in "Todesfuge" are an extension of
this Biblical allusion and "Widerruf" within the context of the
entire collection.

The poem which immediately precedes "Corona" is "Spät
und tief," which was briefly discussed above. Götz Wienold has
succinctly described one of the prevalent themes of the latter
poem, and one which forms a link with "Corona":

"Spät und tief" proclaims the impossibility of the Resurrection. For
this reason the speakers patiently allow the guilt of blasphemy to be
attributed to them, with the words from the Bible with which
Jerusalem let the blood of Christ come upon it. The poem accordingly
reverses the Biblical quotation and suspends the effect of the
Christian symbolism.[12]

The title, "Corona," has many meanings in many different
languages. It is traditionally used as the title of a literary work,
especially a cycle of poems, dealing with Christian themes. For
example, the first of a cycle of seven "Holy Sonnets" by John
Donne is entitled "La Corona." The first line of Donne's poem

is "Deigne at my hands this crown of prayer and praise," and
the poem also contains a reference to other kinds of crowns,
including the crown of thorns. Furthermore, in Donne the word
"corona" also suggests the circular unity of the poetic cycle; the
first line, quoted above, is repeated as the last line of the final
sonnet in the group.[13] Within the Biblical context established in
"Spät und tief," the crown of thorns is one important association suggested by the word "Corona." Several of Celan's subsequent poems refer to this crown, and the allusion in the present
poem provides a further aspect of the "Widerruf." The Biblical
passage in which Christ is mocked and crowned with thorns has
been cited by Joseph Gaer as one of the sources of the legend
of the Wandering Jew. Gaer writes:

"And the soldiers platted a crown of thorns, and put it on his head,
and they put on him a purple robe, and said, Hail King of the
Jews! and they smote him with their hands" ([John] 19:2-3). From
this passage may have come the legendary Cartaphilus who, as we
have seen, dominated all the early legends about the doomed
Wanderer.[14]

Ahasver, the Wandering Jew, has become one of the primary
symbols of the Jewish people through the Christian centuries.
The following quotation from an early source will illustrate
one interpretation which continued to be held by many Christians
until the early part of the present century: "This Wandering
Jew is not a single person, but is rather the entire Jewish people,
which has been scattered throughout the world since the crucifixion of Christ and which, according to Christ's testimony, will
remain homeless until the end of the world."[15] Rilke, in his
"Christus-Visionen," written at approximately the same time as
"Herbsttag," mentions the Wandering Jew in an interesting
context: "So treib ich wie ein welkes Blatt umher./ Kennst du
die Sage von dem ewigen Juden?/ Ich selbst bin jener alte Ahasver" ("Thus do I blow around like a withered leaf. Do you know
the legend of the eternal Jew? I am myself that old Ahasver").
The parallel to the first line of "Herbsttag" is obvious. It is not
unlikely that Celan knew these lines from the "Christus-Visionen,"
or the two poets may have had a common source describing
Ahasver as a blowing leaf.[16]
  The Jews have been persecuted in the name of Christ for

hundreds of years. Now it is time for the wreath of time to be broken; the persecuted Jewish people will no longer accept its fate, which previous generations of Christians and Jews accepted as a matter of course, like the falling of leaves in autumn. The position of "Todesfuge" immediately following "Corona" suggests why it is now finally time. A connection between the two poems is drawn by Siegbert Prawer,[17] and it is only a small step further to tie in the phrase of Richard Rubenstein (quoted above, p. 23); "The roots of the death camps must be sought in the mythic structure of Christianity." The Jews were outcasts for centuries, and for the most part they accepted their fate. But now the tradition has been carried to its logical conclusion. With Auschwitz the limit has been reached. It is time for a change.

Other references to themes relating to religion are present in "Corona." The poem contains allusions to the poetic books of the Old Testament, especially Ecclesiastes, Proverbs, and the Song of Solomon. The modern "es ist Zeit" of "Corona" is, in part, an echo of the Biblical naming of the appropriate times for all endeavors and activities, as in Ecclesiastes 3: "To every thing there is a season, and a time to every purpose under heaven: A time to be born, and a time to die...." In these lines, Celan's two principal sources for "Corona," the Judeo-Christian tradition and Rilke's "Herbsttag," converge. Many of the activities which are listed in Ecclesiastes are also to be found in Celan's poetry. The motif of restlessness coupled with cyclical repetition found in "Corona" is also found in Ecclesiastes: "The wind goeth toward the south, and turneth about unto the north; it whirleth about continually and the wind returneth again according to his circuits." This reminds us of the fact that "Corona" is an endless circle and at the same time evokes the lines from "Herbsttag," "and will wander restlessly in the streets, to and fro, when the leaves are scattered," bringing the motif of the Wandering Jew to mind once more.

As a close examination of the text will reveal, "Corona" contains still other implications, or levels of interpretation. In the first stanza the speaker refers to a close relationship between himself and autumn. The reference to autumn and the leaf immediately calls to mind the use of the words "Herbst" and "Blatt" in the early poem "Schwarze Flocken," where they were associated with the mother's death. The statement "we are friends" would accordingly seem to be ironic. The speaker does, indeed, feel that he is on intimate terms with autumn, but he is hardly pleased with his relationship. The second and third lines indicate that the speaker wishes to make time move, thereby causing autumn, with its unpleasant memories, to pass by. But time refuses to move; autumn remains stationary for the speaker, being always in his memory. Nuts, the fruit of autumn, usually carry unfavorable connotations in Celan, as they do in the present context. Time goes back into the shell; things will apparently continue as they have been, for the speaker as an individual and for the Jews collectively. The use of the image of the shell in a negative context is based upon the cabala. One metaphor for evil which became prominent in later cabalism is, in the words of Gershom Sholem, "that which considers evil as the *Kelipah*, or the 'bark' of the cosmic tree or the 'shell' of the nut."[18]

In the second stanza, the mirror reflects Sunday, the day the Christians associate with the Resurrection of Christ—a motif suggesting the beginning of the modern persecution of the Jews, which is continued from "Spät und tief." A further significance of Sunday can be seen in the religious beliefs and practices of some groups of Eastern Jews. The Messiah was awaited on every Sabbath. Sunday, the following day, was always a day of sadness and mourning because the Messiah had not come on the preceding day. Sunday, then, is the reflected state of the evil world as seen in the mirror. The mirror is associated in Jewish lore, for example, in the cabala, with the condition of the Jewish people. There are two different mirrors; in the one the ultimate supreme God, in the other a manifestation of evil is reflected, for God's larger plan can't be seen. In "Corona," the latter mirror is suggested, and again we see a reversal; something has been turned inside out. The Sabbath has been turned to Sunday, an indication of the ascendancy of Christianity. The God whose reflection is suggested by the word Sunday is the God of the Christians, who are responsible for the persecution of the Jews. The choice of the word Sunday, instead of "Christ" or "Lord," points to the Christian church rather than to the historical Jesus, since it was the early church, and not Jesus, that changed the Sabbath and initiated the persecutions. The second line of the stanza is reminiscent of a passage from "Edgar Jené und der

Traum vom Traume" where sleep and dreams are associated with true insight. The speaker, in this condition, is, accordingly, able to see deeply and thus can speak the "truth," which is now not pleasant. This stanza continues a description of the present time which must be overcome.

In the third stanza, the *ich* has a beloved. Much of the vocabulary of this stanza has erotic overtones. On the simplest level, the speaker and his beloved are bound together by their erotic experiences. They communicate in cipher-like ways known only to themselves and say dark things to each other. Their love encompasses both memory and forgetfulness and produces a synthesis out of which the future will come, provided that the old circle is broken. They are not oblivious to the sufferings of the past—dark things, blood, and wine (a word play with "weinen," "to weep," is present here, as often in Celan and other Jewish writers) contain within them partially negative connotations. But these lovers can perhaps overcome the past. There is a significant ambiguity in the first line of the stanza which points to another level of meaning. The phrase "Geschlecht der Geliebten" most naturally would mean "sex of the beloved woman," but could also mean, taking "Geliebten" to be plural, "race of the beloved people," the Jewish people. This again calls to mind the Old Testament, specifically the Song of Solomon, where erotic imagery is used in contexts which are ultimately religious. Celan's frequent use of erotic imagery for describing the Jewish people can undoubtedly be traced to the double meaning of "Geschlecht" as well as to the applicable Biblical passages.

The next stanza begins with one long dactylic line which emphasizes the bond between the lovers, who are together in the window and thus have a house, unlike the person in the poem "Herbsttag." The rest of the world expressed in "sie sehen uns zu von der Straße" is perhaps the unsympathetic "they" of the preceding poem, "Spät und tief." The window suggests another parallel to Eastern Judaic lore similar to the mourning which took place on Sunday because the Messiah had not come on the previous day. The window is an important symbol in Hassidism, as can be seen in the story "Am Fenster" related by Martin Buber. In the story a rumor that the Messiah has come is circulating and reaches the ears of Rabbi Menachem. The wise rabbi stands in the window, "looks out into the world and says: 'there is no regeneration.' "[19] Again the situation in the poem constitutes a reversal; there is a change in the world, but it has come from within the speaker—considered both as an individual and in his relationship to the Jewish people as a whole. It is now time for the unrest to cease; for the stone to bloom; for the Wandering Jew to be allowed to "build a house." This historical process must be reversed.

The rhythm of the poem, as always in Celan, closely corresponds to the succession of thought and emotion. The long, flowing dactylic rhythm of the first stanza is replaced by a series of short lines, each consisting of a single image which is, at first glance, apparently autonomous. The growing impatience of the speaker is emphasized by this device. The rhythm of the third stanza is again smoother, suggesting the hope promised by the relationship with the beloved—the lover and the Jewish people. Impatience is, once more, suggested in the final lines, especially by the repetitions of the phrase "Es ist Zeit." The final line is set apart as a separate stanza, emphasizing the urgency of the statement. The alternation of emotions between patience and impatience, hope and frustration, finds adequate expression in the complex shifts of rhythm within the poem.

V "Todesfuge"

The impatience and the urgency present in the final lines of "Corona" are clearly explained by the next poem, "Todesfuge."

Schwarze Milch der Frühe wir trinken sie abends
wir trinken sie mittags und morgens wir trinken sie nachts
wir trinken und trinken
wir schaufeln ein Grab in den Lüften da liegt man nicht eng
Ein Mann wohnt im Haus der spielt mit den Schlangen der schreibt
der schreibt wenn es dunkelt nach Deutschland dein goldenes Haar Margarete
er schreibt es und tritt vor das Haus und es blitzen die Sterne er pfeift seine Rüden herbei
er pfeift seine Juden hervor lässt schaufeln ein Grab in der Erde
er befiehlt uns spielt auf nun zum Tanz

Schwarze Milch der Frühe wir trinken dich nachts
wir trinken dich morgens und mittags wir trinken dich abends
wir trinken und trinken
Ein Mann wohnt im Haus und spielt mit den Schlangen der
         schreibt
der schreibt wenn es dunkelt nach Deutschland dein goldenes
         Haar Margarete
Dein aschenes Haar Sulamith wir schaufeln ein Grab in den
         Lüften da liegt man nicht eng

Er ruft stecht tiefer ins Erdreich ihr einen ihr andern singet
         und spielt
er greift nach dem Eisen im Gurt er schwingts seine Augen
         sind blau
stecht tiefer die Spaten ihr einen ihr andern spielt weiter zum
         Tanz auf

Schwarze Milch der Frühe wir trinken dich nachts
wir trinken dich mittags und morgens wir trinken dich abends
wir trinken und trinken
ein Mann wohnt im Haus dein goldenes Haar Margarete
dein aschenes Haar Sulamith er spielt mit den Schlangen

Er ruft spielt süßer den Tod der Tod ist ein Meister aus
         Deutschland
er ruft streicht dunkler die Geigen dann steigt ihr als Rauch
         in die Luft
dann habt ihr ein Grab in den Wolken da liegt man nicht eng

Schwarze Milch der Frühe wir trinken dich nachts
wir trinken dich mittags der Tod ist ein Meister aus Deutschland
wir trinken dich abends und morgens wir trinken und trinken
der Tod ist ein Meister aus Deutschland sein Auge ist blau
er trifft dich mit bleierner Kugel er trifft dich genau
ein Mann wohnt im Haus dein goldenes Haar Margarete
er hetzt seine Rüden auf uns er schenkt uns ein Grab in der Luft
er spielt mit den Schlangen und träumet der Tod ist ein Meister
         aus Deutschland
dein goldenes Haar Margarete
dein aschenes Haar Sulamith

(Black milk of dawn we drink it in the evening we drink it at noon
and in the morning we drink it at night we drink and we drink we
shovel a grave in the air there one is not confined. A man lives in
the house he plays with the serpents he writes he writes when it grows

dark to Germany your golden hair Margarete he writes it and steps in front of the house and the stars sparkle he whistles his dogs to his side he whistles his Jews to appear has them shovel a grave in the ground he commands us to strike up the music for the dance// Black milk of dawn we drink you at night we drink you in the morning and at noon we drink you in the evening we drink and we drink A man lives in the house he plays with the serpents he writes he writes when it grows dark to Germany your golden hair Margarete Your ashen hair Sulamite we shovel a grave in the air there one is not confined//He calls dig deeper in the ground you over there you others sing and play he reaches for the weapon in his belt he waves it his eyes are blue push the spades deeper you over there you others play on for the dance//Black milk of dawn we drink you at night we drink you at noon and in the morning we drink you in the evening we drink and we drink a man lives in the house your golden hair Margarete your ashen hair Sulamite he plays with the serpents// He calls play death more sweetly death is a master from Germany he calls play the violins more darkly then you will climb into the air as smoke then you will have a grave in the clouds there one is not confined//Black milk of dawn we drink you at night we drink you at noon death is a master from Germany we drink you in the evening and the morning we drink and we drink death is a master from Germany his eye is blue he will hit you with a lead bullet his aim is true a man lives in the house your golden hair Margarete he sets his dogs on us he gives us a grave in the air he plays with the serpents and dreams death is a master from Germany your golden hair Margarete your ashen hair Sulamite.)

The poem is basically a description of a concentration camp, from the perspective of the victims who are the speakers in the poem. It is also a poem of frustrated love. Sulamite represents not only the Jewish people, but also the beloved of each individual speaker. Many of the phrases, especially those relating to the man, the Nazi official, are realistic descriptions of some aspect of the camp, such as "a man lives in the house," "he whistles his dogs to his side," and "in the evening he writes to Germany" (most of the camps were, in fact, outside of Germany). Some of the images describing the atrocities in the camp are slightly distorted but still easily recognizable: "shoveling a grave in the air" refers not only to cremation, but also to the responsibility of the Jewish prisoners for doing the actual physical work involved in keeping the instruments of death functioning. The ashen hair of Sulamite suggests the typical dark color of the hair of the Jews, as well as the effects of the cremation. The references to singing and playing allude to the actual existence of orchestras in some camps. Even a small touch like the change from the plural "eyes" to the singular "eye" (lines 17 and 30) suggests the closing of one of the marksman's eyes in the act of shooting. Other images apparently far removed from the realities of the camp are in fact based on equally real physical objects; the "black milk" which the speakers drink and the commandant's playing "with serpents" suggest, of course, alienation and evil, but also allude to the clouds of smoke issuing from the crematories and to the commandant's whip, respectively.

Dozens of critics have discussed "Todesfuge," some briefly, others quite extensively. The interpretations can be divided into three general categories. One group sees elements of "reconciliation" in the poem. Kurt Bräutigam, after citing Celan's phrase "the poem is . . . under way," asks if " 'Todesfuge' isn't under way to human understanding [Verständigung]? . . . Won't [Sulamite and Margarete] once again extend their hands to each other?"[20] Such an interpretation contradicts the very essence of the life and work of Paul Celan. Hans Mayer has refuted this kind of interpretation, observing: "Whatever [Celan] may have been, he was not sentimental and ready to form friendships [i.e., between Christians and Jews]."[21] A second group of critics concentrates upon the aesthetic aspect. Some of them praise the poem as a masterpiece, usually making an observation to the effect that while the poem does not necessarily suggest any reconciliation between the Germans and the Jews, it does, nonetheless, elevate the actual terrors of Auschwitz through the sublimating powers of art. Others would agree that "Todesfuge" sublimates and artistically transforms the terrors of the concentration camps and for this reason condemn the poem; in the famous phrase of Adorno, it is "barbaric" to write (beautiful) poems after Auschwitz.[22]

I prefer a third view regarding the basic significance of "Todesfuge." The poem is indeed beautiful, and its beauty rests in its tremendous power and is accordingly kin to that of Sophocles' *Oedipus Rex* or Picasso's "Guernica." No transcendence is suggested in the poem itself, although its position between "Corona" and "Auf Reisen" mitigates the otherwise inevitable implication of passive acceptance on the part of the speakers. Celan's descriptions of the pictures in "Edgar Jené und der Traum vom Traume" again come to mind. Jené's paintings from the years 1945 to 1948 are, at the same time, beautiful and terrible, in much the same manner as "Todesfuge." But to Celan's way of thinking, this kind of "irrational" interpretation of reality is truer than that given by statistics or "objective" sociological studies. The essence of Auschwitz, and of life, Celan would argue, is more faithfully portrayed by Jené's paintings or by "Todesfuge" than by the statistical statement "6,000,000 Jews were killed by the Nazis." Art captures the terrible reality of the fact, which the objective statement simply fails to convey.

Recently, a number of critics have pointed out Biblical allusions in "Todesfuge." Wolfgang Menzel cites several, including Lamentations 4: 6-8: "For the punishment of the iniquity of the daughter of my people is greater than the punishment of the sin of Sodom. . . . Her Nazarites . . . were whiter than milk. . . . Their visage is blacker than a coal."[23] L. L. Duroche points out that "Psalm 137:1-4 provides us with an example from Jewish history of Jews being forced by their captors to play while under persecution," and goes on to speak of the repetitive nature of the persecution of the Jews through the ages.[24] Dieter Lotze quotes at length from the Song of Solomon; especially significant is 3:6: "Who is this that cometh out of the wilderness like pillars of smoke."[25] Many other references to Biblical passages could be pointed out. Isaiah 4:5 seems to offer a definite model for the poem: "And the Lord will create upon every dwelling place of mount Zion, and upon her assemblies, a cloud and smoke by day, and the shining of a flaming fire by night: for upon all the glory shall be a defence." Isaiah 4 is interpreted as a prophecy of the coming of Christ. All of the allusions to the Bible point in the direction of a "Widerruf" and suggest, ironically, that God's promises to Israel have not been kept.

Much of the vocabulary and imagery of the poem is based on religious and, especially, Biblical symbolism. The unusual word "Erdreich," literally "kingdom of earth," occurs often in the Bible. It suggests the opposite of "Himmelreich," "kingdom of heaven," and its use constitutes an ironic reference to such passages as "Blessed are they which are persecuted for righteousness' sake: for theirs is the kingdom of Heaven" (Matt. 5:10).

The reference to the "Meister," whose home is in Germany, likewise calls the Bible to mind, the passages, for example, when Jesus is addressed by two disciples of John the Baptist, "Rabbi (which is to say, being interpreted, Master) where dwellest thou?" or by Nathanael, "Rabbi, thou art the Son of God, thou art the King of Israel" (John 1:38 and 49). The word "Master" is also used repeatedly in more recent Jewish writings, e.g., the stories of Martin Buber, to refer to the wise teacher or rabbi. In "Todesfuge" the only reality—redeemer and teacher—is death, and it comes from Germany. "Milk," as Menzel observes, "the symbol of clarity, fertility, purity in the Old Testament, has become black in 'Todesfuge.'"[26] Clouds have a positive conotation in the Bible, as Dorothea Forstner has pointed out: "The Lord himself has, in the Old Testament, made the cloud a true and holy symbol; it is the seat and the visible sign of his presence. . . . The cloud in which Jahwe concealed himself is a *prefiguration of the presence of the Lord in the New Covenant.*"[27] Again the Biblical situation is reversed; in "Todesfuge" the cloud is an indication of God's absence, and of the emptiness of the New Covenant. "Blue," to quote Forstner again, is "the color of God"; it was "supposed to remind the Israelites of the God of heaven."[28] But blue is now the color of the Aryan German, who is death personified.

The name Sulamite is also Biblical; it refers to the beautiful woman in the Song of Solomon; "Return, return, O Shulamite; return, return, that we may look upon thee. . . . The hair of thine head [is] like purple" (6:13 and 7:5). Celan's Sulamite cannot return; her beautiful shining hair has been burned to ashes. The significance of the name Margarete is more complex. She is the beloved of the Nazi official and has a "typical" German name, the name of the first love of Goethe's Faust. There is irony in this allusion. Faust's lover Margarete, or Gretchen, was executed for killing her baby; she is both lover and mother. In "Todesfuge" Margarete is only the lover, as the sensual implications of "your golden hair" indicate. Sulamite, on the other hand, would seem to assume both roles in the poem. The parallel to Margarete suggests that she is the lover, yet the reference to ashen hair is by no means sensual, and the repetitions of the word "milk" is suggestive of motherhood. Goethe's Gretchen, justly condemned to death for her murder, is nonetheless "saved" at the end of the drama. Sulamite, on the other hand, is unjustly condemned, but for her there is no salvation. Margarete, the typical German name, also has significance as a Christian symbol, based upon the meaning of the word in Greek: "pearl." Dorothea Forstner discusses this symbol at length, citing many instances of it in Christian writers; for example, one who maintains that "the pearl symbolizes the Logos."[29] Margarete accordingly represents and unites German and Christian as she stands in opposition to the Jewish Sulamite.

The title literally means "Fugue of Death," and some critics see an additional meaning suggested by a word play on the German "Fuge," which is pronounced much like the Latin "fuga," "flight." This second meaning is a further aspect of the Biblical "Widerruf." Lotze draws a parallel to the Song of Solomon 8:14 which, in the German version, begins: "Flee, my friend."[30] The victims, of course, are unable to flee, except as smoke into the air. The fugue is a complicated musical form. Several attempts have been made to adapt individual sections and even phrases of the poem to fit the precise theoretical demands of the form, but none is entirely satisfactory. It can, however, be said with certainty that the poem corresponds in a general way to the structure of the fugue, especially in its utilization of counterpoint.

Much of the poem's effect depends upon the constant, often paradoxical, juxtaposition of opposites. Two especially important contrasts are light and dark (the stars glisten, golden hair, moon; black, night, darkens), and up and down (stars, sky, clouds; earth, dig). Sometimes images combine both aspects of the contrast, as in the reference to height and depth in "a grave in the sky," and to dark and light in the metaphor "black milk." The entire poem is pervaded by the connotations of the words "black milk," and the allusion to smoke or clouds in the sky as both the remnants and final resting place of the victims will appear again and again in Celan's poetry. The word "Frühe" first suggests "dawn," associating the beginning of each day in the camp with the same terrible reminder; but the word also means "early in history," and the allusion to earlier times, together with the effect of the limited vocabulary and rhythm of the first lines, suggests the centuries of Jewish suffering, as Duroche has observed: "The never-ending draught of the Black Milk becomes a metaphor for the suffering of the entire Jewish people; from

the days of the Babylonian captivity to the Nazi death camps."[31]
The second five lines describe "a man," the Nazi. An immediate
contrast is established between the civilized and barbaric sides
of his character. He lives in a house and in the evening writes
letters to his beloved. On the other hand, he plays with serpents
and orders graves to be dug. His command to "begin the dance"
grotesquely transforms a cultured activity into an act of bar-
barism. He whistles for his Jews and for his dogs. For him, and
for the Nazis, Jews are not human beings—another theme which
Celan will return to in future poems. The Jews, in fact, are
accorded less respect than the dogs by the Nazi; the verb "her-
beirufen" is neutral, meaning simply to "call [someone or some-
thing] to oneself," whereas "hervorrufen" is often used in the
sense of applauding or cheering and thereby bringing a per-
former back for an encore or curtain call. The irony typical of
the Nazi's attitude toward his victims is indicated in this word,
as well as in the command itself, to play for a dance—for their
own death-dance.

The superficial structure of the second stanza is not so well
ordered as that of the first. Here the first three lines are devoted
to the Jews, the next two to the German, and the final line to the
Jews again. The two opposites come into closer contact, and the
emotional intensity increases somewhat. Two very important
changes in the formulation of the original metaphor should be
noted. Whereas in the first stanza the evening was the first time
of day mentioned, now night is in first position. Furthermore,
the black milk, previously referred to in the third person, is
now addressed directly, "we drink you." Both changes indicate the increasing sense of despair in the poem, and both are
retained in subsequent stanzas. The use of the second person
in addressing the black milk is especially significant, but is
rarely mentioned when critics discuss the identity of the "thou"
in more difficult poems by Celan. The object of address here—
death, perdition, centuries of persecution—is the only reality the
speakers know. Sulamite, mother and lover, is dead, and God,
too, is absent.

The beginning of the third stanza marks another change of
perspective. Following the single line devoted to the Jews, with
which the preceding stanza concluded, all three lines of the third
strophe describe the German. The beginning is abrupt: "He

calls . . ." It is no longer necessary to identify him as the "man" who "lives in the house"; his presence is felt everywhere, and the simple pronoun is accordingly sufficient. Irony can, once again, be detected in the Nazi's commands. He uses the Biblical word "Erdreich" and pointedly speaks of digging graves and playing a dance tune in the same breath. The steadily increasing frenzy is indicated in this stanza by the rapid shifting of the speakers' attention—from the commands (first "dig," then "play"), to the man's weapon, to his eye, and back to the commands. The fourth stanza begins with the three-line repetition of "Black milk . . . ," then shifts abruptly to the German in the fourth line. The transitions become increasingly disjointed. The phrase "a man lives in the house" is immediately followed by "your golden hair"; the necessary connecting phrase "he writes" is omitted. The perspective of the first half of the fifth line shifts back to the Jews, but then suddenly returns to the German.

The fifth stanza, like the third, contains three lines, all of which describe the man. His irony is again apparent. He tells his victims to play death "sweetly"; he generously promises them a grave in the air where they will not be confined, alluding to a German expression, "das enge Haus" ("the narrow house"), for the grave. He seems to refer mockingly to Isaiah 4:5 when he uses the words "smoke" and "clouds"; he is reminding the Jews of the unfulfilled promises of the Old Testament. He tells them to play the violins "more darkly," suggesting the color of the milk, the nights, and the ashen hair of Sulamite. The word death appears for the first time in the poem; "Tod," with its long "o" sound, ominously occurs twice in close succession. Violins, often associated with death, are likewise mentioned specifically for the first time, making the reference to playing music even more threatening. In general, the language becomes more and more immediately and obviously related to death.

The sixth and final stanza is the longest and most complicated. Like the first, second, and fourth stanzas, it begins with "Black milk . . ." and brings the Jews into even closer proximity with the man and his commands. The first one and one-half lines are devoted to the victims. The sudden interruption of the refrain-like metaphor in the second half of the second line by the phrase "death is a master from Germany" reveals just how close the speakers are to the man, or to death. The metaphor is resumed

and completed in the third line. A further indication of the degree
of intensity now present is the lack of a line division before the
final "we drink and we drink"; three times before these words
had constituted a separate line. The next two lines are rhymed,
a further indication of the increasing intensity of emotion. The
speakers now observe that the man's eye is blue, for one eye is
closed as he aims and prepares to kill them. Lines four through
seven repeat, in rapid succession, the basic activities and attributes of the man which have been mentioned previously in the
poem, suggesting the rapid succession of images from the past
which are often said to flash through the mind of a person at the
time of death.

The speakers, are, indeed, at the point of death, as Celan's
oral interpretation of the poem, available on the record *Lyrik
der Zeit II*, demonstrates.[32] His voice gradually increases in
intensity throughout the poem, especially in the first lines of the
final stanza. It then becomes slower and more dream-like, especially in the eighth line: "er spielt mit den Schlangen und
träumet," where the presence of an extra syllable in "träumet"
suggests a slowing down and a decrease in intensity. The gas
begins to take effect; the speakers, following the panic of antici-
pating death, drift into their final sleep. The last two lines are
spoken by the victims and are their final words, their final comment. The only possible comment is a simple linking of Sulamite
and Margarete—Christian German and Jew. The form of the
lines resembles that of an epigram, and here, as so often, the epi-
grammatic form heightens the contrast between the two different
parts, the distant, but real, beloved woman and the home of
the German on the one hand, and the Jews' lot of broken homes,
lost loved ones, and death on the other. Menzel aptly cites the
Song of Solomon: "The final line of 'Todesfuge' is a remembrance
of love and at the same time a gesture of mourning. 'Love,' says
the Song of Solomon, 'is a flame of the Lord, so that much
water cannot extinguish it, nor rivers engulf it' (8:6-7)."[33] The
Jewish love has been extinguished, the Lord's flame is now
ashes.

CHAPTER 4

Von Schwelle zu Schwelle

I *General Characteristics*

V ON SCHWELLE ZU SCHWELLE (*From Threshold to Threshold,* 1955) marks a subtle but significant break in Celan's lyrical work. The change in direction which can sometimes be detected in the latter part of *Mohn und Gedächtnis* is now made unmistakably clear. Only two of Celan's many collections of poetry contain dedications, and both indicate the author's attitude at the time of publication. *Von Schwelle zu Schwelle* is dedicated to Celan's wife, Gisèle, a Frenchwoman who had no knowledge of German, no interest in German literature, and no affinity to Judaism. The poems in the book consistently, if not completely without exception, display a turning away from veiled personal statements relating to the past and reveal a hesitant search for new values. Each of the three cycles in the book points forward and implies a degree of hope: "Sieben Rosen später," "Mit wechselndem Schlüssel," and "Inselhin" ("Seven Roses Later," "With Changing Key," and "Toward the Island").

Many changes in style and vocabulary can be observed when *Von Schwelle zu Schwelle* is compared with *Mohn und Gedächtnis.* The long dactylic lines of the earlier collection for the most part disappear. Lines consisting of a single word— practically non-existent in *Mohn und Gedächtnis*—are not uncommon in the poems contained in the new volume. Rhyme is now used very sparingly, and only for the purpose of achieving a specific effect. Many changes in image patterns can be noted. Most words relating to water ("Wasser," "trinken," "Wellen") decrease substantially in frequency and two, "Brunnen" and "Quell," entirely disappear. Color imagery also sharply decreases, as do words relating to dream and sleep. Other important words which are now less common are "star," "hair," "heart," "rose," and "love." "God" and the weapons, "sword," "dagger," and "knife'"

77

are not mentioned at all in *Von Schwelle zu Schwelle*. Some images, on the other hand, increase in frequency of appearance: "Stein" ("stone") and several words relating to speech, including "Wort," "sprechen," "nennen," and "Lippe" (which to some extent lacks the erotic connotations of the English "lips"), continuing a trend already pronounced in the latter part of *Mohn und Gedächtnis*.

The emerging pattern is strong, and its implications are clear. Images with a strong personal and emotional content decrease, while stone imagery and vocabulary relating to speech (and poetry) increase in frequency. The speaker is attempting to free himself from his personal fate by detaching it from his poetry and, presumably, from his mind. As James K. Lyon has observed, "The farther one progresses chronologically through his [Celan's] poems, the more a specific plant name is replaced by a generic term."[1] The relationship of the phenomenon described by Lyon to Celan's changing perspective can be seen when the poem "Espenbaum" (MG, 15) is recalled. There, the specific objects— the aspen tree, the dandelion, the oaken door—were automatically associated with the dead mother. Now specific plants, like emotionally charged terms such as "heart" and "love," are removed from the poetry as the speaker attempts to move further away from the emotional impact of the past.

The depersonalization of the poems in *Von Schwelle zu Schwelle* in contrast to those of the earlier *Mohn und Gedächtnis* is also reflected in the use of pronouns. The second person singular, "du," appears with about equal frequency in the two volumes, whereas the first person singular, "ich," is used only about half as often, and the first person plural—the "we Jews" of "Todesfuge"— only about one-quarter as often as in the previous collection. Johannes Firges has aptly described the phenomenon: "[In *Mohn und Gedächtnis*] one often encounters a perplexed "I," which has not yet achieved the distance often attained [in *Von Schwelle zu Schwelle*]."[2] Although it is clear that the speaker is moving away from the entire emotional complex of the past (holocaust, mother, Judaism, Christianity), the goal remains indefinite and can only be expressed in images, such as the island named in the title of the final cycle of the volume, "Toward the Island."

There are but three direct references to religion in *Von*

Schwelle zu Schwelle, all of them occurring in the cycle "Mit wechselndem Schlüssel," and indicating, as the title of the cycle itself suggests, an awareness of the change in emphasis taking place in Celan's poetry. The first of these references is found in the poem "Aufs Auge gepfropft" ("Grafted to the Eye," SS, 30). "Der Ewige pflügt,/ der Herr.// Lausche der Pflugschar, lausche./ Lausche: sie knirscht/ über der harten, der hellen, der unvordenklichen Träne" ("The Eternal One plows, the Lord. Listen to the plow, listen. Listen: it scrapes over the hard, the bright, the immemorial tear"). Here the Lord is not able to penetrate; he fails to make an impression on the tear, for the speaker has successfully hardened himself.

The second reference to religion occurs in "Assisi," (SS, 32), a poem that contains numerous allusions to the life of St. Francis. The lines "Umbrische Nacht mit dem Silber von Glocke und Ölblatt./ Umbrische Nacht mit dem Stein, den du hertrugst" ("Umbrian night with the silver of bell and olive leaf. Umbrian night with the stone which you carried here"), allude to the original calling of the saint by God. One day, a biographer reports, when Francis was in a chapel praying before the crucifix,

it seemed to him that the painted figure spoke, giving a charge to him: "My house is being destroyed; go therefore and repair it for Me." Round him he saw the old chapel, dilapidated and crumbling. . . . And Francis . . . first conceived of his work as the literal task of repairing the chapel.[3]

Some accounts of this event specifically speak of the carrying of stones to repair the chapel. Celan is suggesting that whatever may have become of the chapel, the Church, to which God referred, remains as much in need of repair as ever.

The second of the three pairs of stanzas making up the poem refers to an earthen pot and its maker: "Irdener Krug, dran die Töpferhand festwuchs./ Irdener Krug, den die Hand eines Schattens für immer verschloß" ("Earthen pot, with which the hand of the potter became one. Earthen pot, which the hand of a shadow closed forever"). One allusion here is to St. Francis's skill as a potter and perhaps to the following event in his life:

Once, when he was praying, his eyes fell on a pot he had been making, for he had some skill in that, and his thoughts flew back to some problem in connection with it; but when he had finished praying, he threw it into the fire, saying, "Let us be ashamed of trivial fancies when we are speaking to the great King."[4]

A further allusion is to the common Biblical image of God as potter and his creation—including man—as a pot,[5] an image which Celan combines with another Biblical reference: "in the shadow of his hand hath he [the Lord] hid me. . . . And said unto me, Thou art my servant, O Israel, in whom I will be glorified" (Isa. 49:2f.).

The third pair of stanzas refers to a gray animal, probably a donkey, which suggests Francis's poverty and humility, as well as his intimacy with the world of animals. Much of the vocabulary used throughout the poem, "Stein," "Schatten," "Wort," is indicative of the "new" vocabulary of *Von Schwelle zu Schwelle* and, accordingly, suggests poetic creation. The final couplet connects this theme with that of the inadequacy of Christianity:

> Glanz, der nicht trösten will, Glanz.
> Die Toten—sie betteln noch, Franz.

(Brilliance, which does not want to console, brilliance. The dead— they are still begging, Francis.)

Francis of Assisi—with whom the word "Glanz" is often connected by his biographers—represents the best the Christian tradition has to offer, and it is said to be inadequate. The dead—the Jewish victims—are not helped by Francis's virtues. "Glanz" and related words, according to Lyon, "occur in at least eleven poems, each time as an image connected with speech."[6] It would, accordingly, seem that the poet is here questioning the success of his new mode of expression as well as that of Francis's attempted revitalization of the Church. He seems to find no consolation in the splendor of his words created at the cost of his forgotten or repressed relationship with his mother and the other victims of the holocaust. The poem "Assisi" is probably a "Widerruf" of a specific source from literature, the visual arts, or a biography of St. Francis. I have been unable to locate this source, which, if indeed it does exist, would combine the important images used by Celan in the poem.

The third of the three poems referring to religion is "Vor einer Kerze" ("Before a Candle," SS, 34f.). It, too, combines elements of the new vocabulary with powerful emotional elements which encompass both direct personal references to the dead mother—the only such instance in the entire collection—and the extensive use of religious imagery. The speaker in the poem is situated in front of a candle—an important object in Jewish ritual —located in a candelabrum which he formed according to the mother's instructions. A blessing is spoken:

Im Namen der drei, . . ./Im Namen des ersten der Drei,/der aufschrie,/als es zu leben galt dort, wo vor ihm sein Wort schon gewesen,/im Namen des zweiten, der zusah und weinte,/im Namen des dritten, der weiße/Steine häuft in der Mitte,—/sprech ich dich frei/vom Amen, . . .

(In the name of the three . . . In the name of the first of the Three who cried out when the issue was life, there, where his word was before him, in the name of the second, who watched and wept, in the name of the third, who heaps up white stones in the center, I absolve you of the amen.)

The attributes of the three persons of the Trinity are given metaphorically in vocabulary typical of Celan. The Holy Spirit, the inspiration and divine source of the Word of God, is described as the one who piles up stones, suggesting verbal communication (as in "Assisi" and "Welchen der Steine du hebst," to be discussed below). The attributes of Jesus, watching and weeping, are reminiscent of his passion and his prediction of the destruction of Jerusalem. The attribute of God, the Father mentioned here is an allusion to John 1, "In the beginning was the Word . . . and the Word was God." The Trinity of the Christian prayer is irreverently introduced in this Jewish prayer, in the process of absolving the thou of the amen. In this poem Celan once again refuses to place the stamp of approval—here the amen—on a prayer; he will not say "Thy Will be done."[7]

As Siegbert Prawer has observed, *Von Schwelle zu Schwelle* "has more self-reflecting, inturned poems, more poems about poetry" than the previous collection.[8] The "word" is a complicated phenomenon, and in this collection Celan seems to be struggling for a satisfactory relation to it. Celan's word is not simply the

poetic word common to much poetry about poetry, but it has
many connotations which derive from religious sources. Thus it
may refer to the "logos" mentioned by John. "Logos" is not a
simple term. In classical times, it incorporated the "rationality
of the Greeks"; it represented and expressed "rational, correct
judgment." The meaning changes in Christian times, when "God
is present in the logos; whoever sees the incarnate logos, sees
the Father."[9] Jesus is the "Word made Flesh." The primacy of
the Word in the Christian New Testament implies a denial of the
Ruach of the Old Testament, "And the Spirit [*Ruach, voice*]
of God moved upon the face of the waters" (Gen. 1:2). Peter
Mayer has added a further aspect to the significance of the "word"
in Celan. He explicitly equates it with Judaism: "*One* word is
consistently paraphrased, evaded, sought...the word, 'you
know: a corpse' [a quote from SS, 49], the word Jew."[10]

The first poem of *Von Schwelle zu Schwelle*, "Ich hörte sagen"
("I heard it said," SS, 9), refers to the word and is in many
respects programmatic: "Ich hörte sagen, es sei/ im Wasser ein
Stein und ein Kreis/ und über dem Wasser ein Wort,/ das den
Kreis um den Stein legt." ("I heard it said that there was a
stone and a circle in the water and over the water a word which
forms the circle around the stone"). This passage incorporates
the "word" of John into a passage strongly reminiscent of Genesis,
thereby alluding to the ascendancy of Christianity. There is a further reference here to a Jewish myth according to which the
world began when God threw a stone into the water.[11] But the
allusions are veiled, and the remainder of the poem—from the
fifth line, "I saw my poplar go down to the water," to the last,
"And saw my poplar no more"—is quite different, suggesting the
break which takes place in the poet's expressed concern with
Judaism and his Jewish past. The poplar, which he no longer
sees, may be his dead mother.

The first poem of the final cycle, "Nächtlich geschürzt"
("Nightly girded," SS, 49f.), likewise contains an important
reference to the word. Its final lines are:

> Ein Wort—du weißt:
> eine Leiche.
> Laß uns sie waschen,
> laß uns sie kämmen,

laß uns ihr Aug
himmelwärts wenden.

(A word—you know: a corpse. Let us wash it, let us comb it, let
us turn its eye toward heaven.)

Lyon perceptively interprets the passage as "an imperative to
the poet to 'prepare the body' for speech in the same manner
that the women prepared Christ's body prior to resurrection."[12]
God, Christ, the Word made Flesh, is dead, says the poet, and
a new value must be sought. The dead word suggests Christ's
dead body and in addition carries the implication that the
poetic word, when revived, will seek a new, unspecified
transcendence. The *Ruach* gave way to the *logos,* and now the
Word is dead, hopefully to be replaced by something better.
Here we see very clearly a vindication of Prawer's statement,
made about the poem "Psalm": "This is the language of a natural
God-seeker who has failed to find God, yet cannot leave off
calling into nothingness and emptiness in the hope of an
answer."[13] The attitude of hope is maintained in the poem which
immediately follows "Nächtlich geschürzt," "Auge der Zeit"
("Eye of Time," SS, 51): "Es wird warm in der Welt,/ und die
Toten/ knospen und blühen" ("It grows warm in the world and
the dead bud and blossom"). The pattern is unmistakable. *Von
Schwelle zu Schwelle* represents an attempt, generally successful,
to turn away from many aspects of the past—from the snow of
"Edgar Jené und der Traum vom Traume" and the smoke of
"Todesfuge"—and grope toward a new transcendence.

Critical opinion is divided regarding the poems of this collection. They are often praised on account of the compactness of
language, especially vis-à-vis that of *Mohn und Gedächtnis.* But
I feel that the poems of *Von Schwelle zu Schwelle,* with a very
few notable exceptions, are among the least successful written
by Celan in the period 1945 to 1964. They often seem artificial
and contrived; the depth of feeling present in the early poems is
missing, and little of compensatory value has been added. The
collection serves as a transitional stage between *Mohn und
Gedächtnis* and *Sprachgitter,* but for the most part it lacks the
extraordinary power of the latter as well as the former work.

II   "Mit wechselndem Schlüssel"

I have selected three poems for interpretation, each of which
deals with Celan's new perspective of the creative process and
his relation to it. The first is the title poem of the middle cycle,
"Mit wechselndem Schlüssel" (SS, 36).

> Mit wechselndem Schlüssel
> schließt du das Haus auf, darin
> der Schnee des Verschwiegenen treibt.
> Je nach dem Blut, das dir quillt
> aus Aug oder Mund oder Ohr,
> wechselt dein Schlüssel.
>
> Wechselt dein Schlüssel, wechselt das Wort,
> das treiben darf mit den Flocken.
> Je nach dem Wind, der dich fortstößt,
> ballt um das Wort sich der Schnee.

(With changing key you unlock the house, in which the snow of
that which is kept silent is blowing. According to the blood which
flows from your eye or mouth or ear, your key changes.//If the key
changes, the word which is allowed to blow with the flakes will
change. According to the wind which drives you away, the snow
hardens around the word.)

In this poem the poet is addressing himself.[14] Roughly, the
house represents his consciousness and the "Schnee des Verschwiegenen," his bitter experiences, his memories of these experiences, and the need to "speak" of them (to come to terms with
them). The changing key refers to his own approach to the problem, which, as can be seen in the poetry, is changing from a fairly
direct emotional response to what is essentially an attempt to
sublimate or repress. The nature of the response—the changing of
the key—depends on the relationship of his suffering to his perception and the world. In the Jené essay Celan touches upon
the necessity of rearranging the normal modes of sense perception. The mouth, he says, approaches truth more readily than the
eyes which are bound to a visible, rational, and therefore
untrustworthy reality. Only when the eyes are moved to the
breast, thereby becoming agents of the heart rather than the
brain, of emotion rather than reason, do they effectively function
as transmitters of truth. In the poem, however, the alternation of

the senses is mentioned without the optimism expressed in the early essay; the speaker is no longer confident that he has found the answer.

"If the key changes, the word which is allowed to blow with the flakes will change." The word, the poem, is completely dependent upon the emotional attitude of the poet, which is the key.[15] The speaker's lack of any conscious control once the process is set in motion is expressed in the final two lines. The word order of the last line is somewhat unusual and offers striking confirmation of the interpretation given above. Although no hard-and-fast rule of grammar is broken, a more normal pattern would be "ballt sich der Schnee um das Wort," in which case the poem would close with a hard sound and the fixed meaning of the word "Wort." But even though the stress pattern of the two constructions is identical, the less common one is selected. The poem accordingly concludes with the open diphthong of the word "Schnee," which parallels the open, metaphoric meaning of the line and of the poem. The entire tone of the poem is one of questioning uncertainty; the statements are simple, and the rhythm is slow and somewhat uneven.

III "Welchen der Steine du hebst"

The second poem to be discussed is "Welchen der Steine du hebst" (SS, 53), from the cycle "Inselhin."[16]

> Welchen der Steine du hebst—
> du entblößt,
> die des Schutzes der Steine bedürfen:
> nackt,
> erneuern sie nun die Verflechtung.
>
> Welchen der Bäume du fällst—
> du zimmerst
> die Bettstatt, darauf
> die Seelen sich abermals stauen,
> als schütterte nicht
> auch dieser
> Äon.
>
> Welches der Worte du sprichst—
> du dankst
> dem Verderben.

(Whichever stone you lift—you lay bare those who need the protection of the stones: naked, they now renew their intertwining.//
Whichever tree you fell—you build a bed, upon which the souls
pile up again, as if this aeon did not also tremble.//Whichever word
you speak—you owe to perdition.)

The image of lifting stones, it will be recalled, is associated with
speech in Celan's poetry. The present poem is probably the
clearest evidence of this symbolism. The first line of the final
stanza is parallel to the first lines of the preceding stanzas, in
meaning as well as in structure: lifting stones, felling trees, and
speaking words are equated. The final stanza is the key to the
poem. Peter Mayer has explained the significance of these
enigmatic lines: "Celan wrote exclusively in German, in the
language of death, which was a 'Master from Germany.' Each
line is accordingly painful memory by virtue of the language in
which it is written. And in addition to being painful memory, it
is also necessity. 'Whichever word you speak—you owe to perdition.'"[17] This stanza calls to mind Celan's association of "denken"
and "danken" in his Bremen speech. He owes his poetry to the
German language, and he must think of Germany when he
writes. The irony of thanking the Germans for anything—and
of owing them anything—surely has not escaped him, either in
the poem or in the speech.

The images of the poem are suggested by a Biblical passage:
"Whoso removeth stones shall be hurt therewith; and he that
cleaveth wood shall be endangered thereby.... The words of a
wise man's mouth are gracious; but the lips of a fool will swallow
up himself" (Ecc. 10:9 and 12). The initial line of each stanza
refers to this Biblical passage. Each is followed by a dash,
indicating the transition to a personal frame of reference. The
speaker is, indeed, "hurt" by speaking, but he doubts the validity
of the Biblical distinction between the words of a wise man and
a fool. The Scriptures are still an important force for Celan, but
the complexities of the present time have first priority, and the
Biblical reference is not developed.

In the first stanza of "Welchen der Steine du hebst," the speaker
refers to himself and to other Jews who are reminded of the
holocaust by the (German) poetry created by lifting the stones.
Here we see the answer to the rhetorical question from the
early poem "Nähe der Gräber": "Und duldest du, Mutter, wie

einst, ach, daheim,/ den leisen, den deutschen, den schmerzlichen Reim?" The answer is a veiled but unambiguous no; but none-theless the poems must be written. The second stanza takes up another image used by Celan in relation to poetic creativity, the felling of trees,[18] and it likewise refers to the reaction of the poet, as a Jew, to his German poetry. It forms a bed, something suggesting peace and rest, "as if this aeon did not also tremble," as if the possibility of peace existed for the millions of victims. One is reminded of the final couplet of "Assisi"—the "Glanz" of poetry does not console the dead; quite the contrary.

IV   "Sprich auch du"

The third and final poem, "Sprich auch du" ("Speak as well," SS, 59), is more optimistic; it looks forward toward the new transcendence, and away from the old memories of hate implicit in "Welchen der Steine du hebst."[19]

> Sprich auch du,
> sprich als letzter,
> sag deinen Spruch.
>
> Sprich—
> Doch scheide das Nein nicht vom Ja.
> Gib deinem Spruch auch den Sinn:
> Gib ihm den Schatten.
>
> Gib ihm Schatten genug,
> gib ihm so viel,
> als du um dich verteilt weißt zwischen
> Mittnacht und Mittag und Mittnacht.
>
> Blicke umher:
> sieh, wie's lebendig wird rings—
> Beim Tode! Lebendig!
> Wahr spricht, wer Schatten spricht.
>
> Nun aber schrumpft der Ort, wo du stehst:
> Wohin jetzt, Schattenentblößter, wohin?
> Steige. Taste empor.
> Dünner wirst du, unkenntlicher, feiner!
> Feiner: ein Faden,
> an dem er herabwill, der Stern:

um unten zu schwimmen, unten,
wo er sich schimmern sieht: in der Dünung
wandernder Worte.

(Speak as well, speak as the last one, utter your saying.//Speak, but
do not divide nay from yea. Give meaning to your saying, give it
the shadow.//Give it shadow enough, give it as much as you know
to be distributed around you between midnight and midday and
midnight.//Look around: see how full of life it is becoming everywhere—By death! full of life! He speaks true who speaks shadow.//
But now the place where you are standing is shrinking: Whither
now, you who are divested of shadows? Climb, grope upwards.
You grow thinner, less recognizable, finer! Finer, a thread, on which
it wants to descend, the star, in order to swim below, below, where
it sees itself shimmer: in the swell of wandering words.)

In the opening stanza, the speaker addresses himself with the
exhortation that he, too, should speak and utter his "Spruch."
One level of meaning present in this difficult poem is based on
an extended Biblical allusion, especially to Genesis and John.
The language is decidedly Biblical: "Spruch" can mean "Proverb,"
and "spricht" is the word used to describe God's acts of creation
in Genesis, "God spoke, let there be light. . . ." God spoke "in the
beginning," to initiate the creation of the world; now the poet
speaks too, "as the last one." The Biblical allusion is confirmed
and expanded in the following stanza: "speak, but do not divide
nay from yea. Give meaning to your saying: give it the shadow"
The divisions described in Genesis, especially the division of
light from darkness, are suggested by these lines; "scheiden" is
the German word used in Luther's translation. Celan's poem
demands that the shadow, the super-imposition of darkness upon
light and, accordingly, the union of light and darkness, be given
to the "Spruch."

The gospel of St. John likewise mentions a division of light
and dark: "And the light shineth in darkness; and the darkness
comprehended it not" (1:5). The Bible frequently alludes to the
separation of "yea" from "nay"; the most significant passage in
the present context of "Sprich auch du" is: "But as God is true,
our word toward you was not yea and nay. For the Son of God,
Jesus Christ, who was preached among you . . . was not yea and
nay, but in him was yea. For all the promises of God in him are
yea" (2 Cor. 1:18-20). Celan denies the light and the "yea" of

Christ, rejecting, once again, the simplicity of the Christian solution.

The third stanza continues the Biblical allusion. Where Genesis repeatedly mentions the morning and the evening, representing the division of night and day, the poem speaks of the span from midnight to midday to midnight, suggesting the continuity between night and day and confirming the poet's resolve to remove the distinction between the two. The first lines of the fourth stanza represent the poet's ironic comment on the account of creation given in Genesis. Just as God looked over his newly created world with its many thriving plants and animals and pronounced it "good," so the poet says "see how full of life it is becoming everywhere." Then, in Genesis, death is introduced almost immediately. The poet's reaction, as he follows the progression, is ironic. He exclaims "By death! Full of life!," expressing his dissatisfaction with the turn of events. His answer, a "Widerruf," follows: the only truth is to be found in shadows, in failing to make sharp, rational distinctions where none actually exist, as between light and dark, yea and nay.

The allusion to Biblical creation establishes the connection with Celan's new concept of poetic creation. The speaker exhorts himself not to allow the "logos" to revert to its original rationalistic meaning. "Shadow" suggests light and dark on a literal level, but in a metaphorical sense it also applies quite naturally to a poetic statement which shuns direct, simplified, rationalistic phrases; hence it is the perfect image for linking the Bible with Celan's own conception of poetic creativity. The poet speaks the truth by giving shadows to his writing. (Shadow, of course, also suggests death.) The final stanza, for the most part, abandons the reference to the Bible and is directed primarily to the poet himself. Having substituted his own creation for that of Genesis, he asks himself: "Wohin jetzt, Schattenentblößter?" The meaning of this phrase is clarified by a reference to a similar expression in "Welchen der Steine du hebst." By creating German poetry which deals with his emotional reactions, Celan has divested himself of the protection afforded by silence. He has now only one path which he can follow; he feels that he must climb upwards, becoming the thread upon which the star can descend to the wandering words.

The star is a twinkling bright spot in the darkness of night, an island, in a sense. Furthermore it is large but appears to be small. Hence it is an apt symbol for "not dividing the nay from the yea." It also represents the Jewish star, the symbol of the Jewish people, and herein lies a final "Widerruf" of the conclusion of the first chapter of John: "Hereafter ye shall see heaven open, and the angels of God ascending and descending upon the Son of man" (1:51). Celan's poetry assumes the mediating role of Christ, and the Jewish dead replace the angels of John's gospel. The star is the new transcendence, the "Other" sought by Celan which the poet hopes to be able to bring down to earth. The words, in which the star will swim, are in motion. They are not fixed or static, but are in a state of flux suggesting the absence of logical rationalistic boundaries. Perhaps the heights of "Sprich auch du" can be contrasted with the "Tiefsee" of "Edgar Jené und der Traum vom Traume." Whereas the poet previously dwelt in the depths, he now desires to climb upward, and in so doing to provide the means by which the star can descend. His path takes him from "Tiefsee" to the stars, from extreme to extreme, from "Schwelle zu Schwelle," and he expresses—in this poem—the hope for a successful synthesis here on earth.

CHAPTER 5

Sprachgitter

I General Characteristics

THE appearance of *Sprachgitter* in 1959 was greeted by almost unanimous critical acclaim, and the book quickly solidified Celan's claim to a position as one of the leading German-speaking poets of the postwar era. The linguistic changes described in the preceding chapter are accelerated in *Sprachgitter,* and the poems, individually and collectively, are more effective. The language continues to grow harder and colder, and the words sparser. Lines consisting of a single word—often an unusual word—are now common. A depth of feeling often missing in the poems of *Von Schwelle zu Schwelle* is consistently and unmistakably present. The book is shorter than *Von Schwelle zu Schwelle,* just as the latter was shorter than *Mohn und Gedächtnis.* It comprises thirty-three poems, including "Stimmen" and "Engführung," the two long ones with which the collection opens and closes. Of the six divisions, or cycles, only the last one, "Engführung," has a title. The first five are identified only by Roman numerals—still another example of the condensation of language in *Sprachgitter* vis-à-vis the earlier collections.

It is difficult to isolate a prevalent theme or direction in the poems of this volume. The ambiguity inherent in the book is reflected in the ambiguity of the title. "Sprachgitter," an unusual combination of the abstract concept "language" with the concrete term "lattice" or "grill," could have several meanings. In his excellent article "Accessus zu Celans 'Sprachgitter,'" Alfred Kelletat suggests four possible meanings of the word: (1) the original, literal one, namely the window through which cloistered nuns were allowed to speak to outsiders; (2) the metaphorical use of the term made by Jean Paul (1763-1825), "The old man ... spoke behind the *Sprachgitter* of sleep with dead persons";

(3) language itself may be a "Gitter" through which ideas are simultaneously realized (through expression) and limited (by the form of the expression); (4) going back to its etymological root, "Gitter" may imply a union or a binding together.[1] A specific modern usage may also be pertinent: "Beugungsgitter" is the technical term for a diffraction grating, an instrument used to filter and order light. The problem may be reduced to a simple question: does Celan's "Gitter" imply bars and fences—and thereby separation and isolation—or does it refer to its etymological root and suggest union and order? The question is a difficult one, and the answer must be based upon an examination of the poems, considered in light of the poet's changing relationship to his Jewish past and his German poetry, and his awareness of this relationship.

A number of passages in the collection refer, more or less directly, to Judaism or Christianity: the "Lord" of "Tenebrae," the thorn and the wound of the "Matière de Bretagne" (which allude to the passion of Christ), the titles of "Tenebrae" and "Allerseelen" (technical terms in the Catholic Church), and the reference to the "Sand people" in the poem "Oben, geräuschlos." Most significantly, the opening and closing poems are constructed around Jewish themes. "Stimmen" ("Voices," SG, 7-9) consists of eight semi-autonomous sections. The first five sections begin with the word "Stimmen"; the sixth, which expressly introduces the Jewish element, with "Jakobsstimme" ("The Voice of Jacob"); the seventh with "Stimmen im Innern der Arche" ("Voices inside the Ark"); and the eighth with "Keine/ Stimme" ("No voice"). The conception of the "Stimme" is unmistakably Jewish, as the following remarks of Hermann Hakel, describing Celan's changing poetic voice, will demonstrate:

Celan turns away from the word, of which he is, of course, the master—in the literary sphere—and seeks the voice. And when I became aware of this direction in his works, I again saw that I was observing a Jew. Jews don't think in terms of language [*Sprache*] but rather in terms of voice [*Stimme*].

In the final stanza, following and corresponding to direct references to the Old Testament in the previous two stanzas, the phrase "No voice" occurs. This voice is then explained by an image, "ein/ Spätgeräusch.../ ein/ Fruchtblatt, augengroß,

tief/ geritzt; es/ harzt, will nicht/ vernarben" ("a late noise
... a carpophyll [part of the female reproductory system of a
plant], large as an eye, deeply cut, it oozes, refuses to cicatrize").
On one level, this would seem to be an explanation of the poet's
condition; he had abandoned his Jewish voice in his earlier
poetry, especially in *Von Schwelle zu Schwelle,* and has come to
experience this as a wound which will not heal. The words also
suggest the absence of God's voice in recent times, an absence
which also has prevented wounds from healing.[2]

The final poem of *Sprachgitter,* unquestionably one of Celan's
finest, is called "Engführung" ("Stretto," SG, 57f.).[3] This piece,
as Peter Mayer observes, "reflects a return of the speaker ... to
the territory in which the holocaust took place." "Stretto" is
defined as "the close overlapping of voices in a fugue, each
beginning very shortly after the preceding one, often the final
section." The connection with "Todesfuge" is obvious, and several critics have commented on it. Hans Mayer once interpreted
"Engführung" as a refutation of "Todesfuge," saying that Celan,
in effect, took back his earlier poem and replaced it with "Engführung," because "Todesfuge" was so often falsely interpreted
as a sign of reconciliation between Christians and Jews. Mayer
later reports that, after reading his interpretation, Celan vigor-
ously rejected his hypothesis, saying: "My dear Hans Mayer, I
never take a poem back."[4] Mayer is surely correct in stating that
"Engführung" is related to the critical reception of "Todesfuge,"
but Celan's statement can also be accepted as valid. If "Engführung" is viewed as a refutation of the many false interpretations of "Todesfuge," rather than of the poem itself, the
apparently irreconcilable standpoints of Mayer and Celan are
easily brought into accord.

The following lines will give an indication of the tone prevalent in the poem as well as illustrate Celan's continuing use of
his favorite words in ambiguous contexts: "Kam, kam./ Kam
ein Wort, kam,/ kam durch die Nacht,/ wollt leuchten, wollt
leuchten.// Asche./ Asche, Asche./ Nacht" ("Came, came. A
word came, came, came through the night, wanted to shine,
wanted to shine. Ash. Ash, ash. Night"). As Peter Mayer points
out in his discussion of this passage, the word alluded to is the
word "Jew." It is also Jesus, the Word made Flesh, who came
"to bear witness of the Light, that all men through him might

believe. . . . That was the true Light, which lighteth [erleuchtet]
every man. . . . He came unto his own, and his own received him
not" (John 1:7, 9, and 11). Now the Jews, the ones who did not
receive Jesus, are ashes, as is the brilliance of the Word and the
brilliance of Christianity.

Another poem which combines a negative tone with religious
imagery is "Matière de Bretagne" (SG, 32f.). The poem begins
with a description of yellow thorn bushes "festering toward
heaven" (the French word *matière* can also mean "fester"). This
is immediately followed by the phrase "the thorn woos the
wound," a reference, as Walter Jens was the first to point out, to
Christ.[5] The tone of the poem is pessimistic. In the third stanza,
the speaker asks "(Kanntet ihr mich,/ Hände? Ich ging/ den
gegabelten Weg, den ihr weist, mein Mund/ spie seinen Schotter,
. . .)" ("Did you know me, hands, I traveled the forked road
which you point out, my mouth spouted its rubble"). The tone and
rhythm of the fourth stanza (in which the images previously used
in the poem are repeated) are reminiscent of "Engführung." The
six lines contain only five different words, repeated in various com-
binations: "Du lehrst deine Hände schlafen" ("You teach your
hands to sleep"). The hands have not been sleeping; they were
busy "pointing out the forked road." This refers to the type of
poetry which Celan has been writing, as well as to his own
state of mind. He is not satisfied with either of them, as the
negative tone of the phrase "Mein Mund/ spie seinen Schotter"
indicates. Now the speaker is teaching the hands to sleep. Sleep
carries the same meaning here as it does in "Edgar Jené und
der Traum vom Traume," suggesting the irrational realm in
which truth can be perceived and appreciated.

By no means are all of the poems in *Sprachgitter* pessimistic,
however. "Blume" ("Flower," SG, 25), for example, expresses
a very hopeful attitude, while utilizing images similar to those
of "Matière de Bretagne." The first line consists of a single phrase,
"Der Stein" ("The stone"), suggesting hardness and, thereby,
a contrast with the softness suggested by the title; this contrast
establishes the basic image pattern of the poem. The second
stanza reads:

> Wir waren
> Hände,

> ... wir fanden
> das Wort, das den Sommer heraufkam:
> Blume.

(We were hands ... we found the word, which came up the summer: flower.)

As Peter Horst Neumann has pointed out, the combination of "darkness" and "word" suggests the first chapter of the gospel of St. John.[6] The final two stanzas bring the flower and the stone together:

> Wachstum.
> Herzwand um Herzwand
> blättert hinzu.
>
> Ein Wort noch, wie dies, und die Hämmer
> schwingen im Freien.

(Growth. Heart-wall by heart-wall leafs nearer. One more word, like this one, and the hammers will swing in the open.)

The key to the significance of the hammers and to the enigmatic relationship of the final image to the remainer of the poem is to be found in the etymology of the word "hammer": the root from which it derives means "stone." Thus if one more word like "flower" is spoken, the stone will become a hammer, swinging freely. Neumann offers two possible meanings for the final image. It may suggest the hammer of a bell, perhaps of the flower "Osterglocke" ("Easter lily"; literally: "Easter bell"), or, following a famous line by Rilke, the reference may also be to the "hammers of the heart." A brief comparison with the close of "Corona" makes both associations plausible and appealing: "It is time that the stone condescended to bloom, that a heart beat for unrest." The poem "Blume," too, alludes to the stone's blooming and the heart's beating freely.

II   "Tenebrae"

But the prevailing tone of *Sprachgitter* is not one of tentative affirmation, as in "Blume." A more typical poem in this respect is "Tenebrae" (SG, 23f.).

Nah sind wir, Herr,
nahe und greifbar.

Gegriffen schon, Herr,
ineinander verkrallt, als wär
der Leib eines jeden von uns
dein Leib, Herr.

Bete, Herr,
bete zu uns,
wir sind nah.

Windschief gingen wir hin,
gingen wir hin, uns zu bücken
nach Mulde und Maar.

Zur Tränke gingen wir, Herr.

Es war Blut, es war,
was du vergossen, Herr.

Es glänzte.

Es warf uns dein Bild in die Augen, Herr.
Augen und Mund stehn so offen und leer, Herr.

Wir haben getrunken, Herr.
Das Blut und das Bild, das im Blut war, Herr.

Bete, Herr.
Wir sind nah.

(We are nigh, Lord, nigh and graspable.//Already grasped, Lord,
twisted together, as though the body of each of us were your body,
Lord.//Pray, Lord, pray to us, we are nigh.//Against the wind we
walked, walked to bend down to the trough and the pond.//We went
to be watered, Lord// It was blood, it was, which you shed, Lord.// It
glistened.//It threw back your image into our eyes, Lord. Eyes and
mouth are so open and empty, Lord.//We have drunk, Lord. The
blood and the image which was in the blood, Lord.//Pray, Lord,
we are nigh.)

"Tenebrae" is a Latin word meaning darkness or night.
Specifically, it is applied to the darkness following the crucifixion. Later, the term came to refer to a service in Holy Week

during which psalms are sung and, one by one, fifteen candles are extinguished until, at the end, only a single candle remains burning. Through the associations of the title a somber mood is evoked, playing on some hidden connections with Christianity, which are to become clear in the course of the poem. But the first lines of the poem evoke still other associations. "Nah sind wir, Herr/ nahe und greifbar" recalls the opening lines of "Patmos," a famous poem by Friedrich Hölderlin (1770-1843), "Nah ist/ Und schwer zu fassen der Gott./ Wo aber Gefahr ist, wächst/ Das rettende auch" ("God is near and difficult to grasp. But where danger is, salvation also grows"). Hölderlin's "schwer zu fassen" refers to the difficulty with which man comprehends God's plan, but the ultimate goodness of God is implicit in the formulation. The poem is, essentially, a word of comfort in dark times, based upon the security of a belief in the presence of a benevolent God in the universe.

In "Tenebrae," on the other hand, reproach and perhaps anger are expressed because God is either absent or his presence in the universe is meaningless: God is no longer good, though hard to comprehend, as in Hölderlin, and the speakers are, therefore, bitter and reproachful. God is not at the present time "salvation in danger." The entire poem, as Götz Wienold has shown, is a carefully structured refutation of "Patmos," containing, in addition, several allusions to the Bible.[7] Among the passages mentioned by Wienold is Psalm 34, which is especially significant in the "Widerruf": "O taste and see that the Lord is good: blessed is the man that trusteth in him. . . . The righteous cry, and the Lord heareth. . . . The Lord is nigh unto them that are of a broken heart" (Ps. 34:8 and 17f.). The speakers, the "we" of the poem, have seen and tasted the Lord, but they have not seen his goodness.

The first half of the second stanza describes a tortured picture. The speakers are "clutched" by some force and twisted up together, suggesting the dying and dead victims of the gas chamber.[8] The second half of the stanza suggests a comparison between these bodies and the body of Christ on the cross. The third stanza then inverts another religious motif; when man approaches death, he draws near to God and prays for the forgiveness of his sins. In the poem, it is God who must pray as the dead draw near, for it is he who has sinned, by failing to keep his promises to save his people in their hour of need.

The third and fourth stanzas suggest drinking. Ruth Lorbe
suggests an additional level of meaning brought into the poem
by the association of Jews with animals.[9] The word "Tränke"
normally refers to a watering place for animals, and not for
human beings. This image, accordingly, simultaneously calls
to mind the theme of Jews as sub-human (familiar in Celan),
and alludes to and distorts the Biblical description of the Lord
as the Good Shepherd. This time the flock has been given blood
to drink by the Shepherd. The words of the Lord in Isaiah 43:20
come to mind: "I give waters in the wilderness, and rivers in
the desert, to give drink to [tränke] my people, my chosen one."
The speakers have now assumed the role of sacrificial lambs.
There is, then, in the poem a double reference to Leviticus 17,
where the laws relating to sacrifice and the consumption of
blood are given: the words "Blut vergossen" ("shed blood")
appear in the fourth verse of that chapter, and the fourteenth
verse contains the admonition that the consumption of blood is
strictly forbidden to the Jews. God has, then, broken two of
his commandments: he has shed blood and given it to his people
to consume.

The blood glistens and assumes mirror-like qualities. When
the speakers look into the mirror, they see their own reflections,
with their own empty eyes and mouths. Here reference is made
to Psalm 34:1, quoted above; neither eye nor mouth has found
satisfaction. It is as though the water hole had been poisoned—
a veiled allusion to the medieval Christian superstition according to which Jews were believed to be responsible for poisoning
wells with, among other things, human blood. The first line of
the eighth stanza indicates that the speakers see the image of
the Lord when they gaze into the mirror-like surface. On the one
hand this suggests that, according to the Bible, man was made
in the image and likeness of God; he should, accordingly,
perceive the presence of God when he examines himself. And
this, indeed, is the case: the features of the Jews (on account
of their unspeakable suffering) and of God (because he allowed
their suffering to happen) are grotesquely distorted. There is
still another implication here. Jesus preached love and mercy,
but all the Jews have received from Christians is blood.

The tone of the poem is unmistakably bitter. Each stanza is

short and concisely formulated. The speakers are perfectly aware of their situation; there is no sign of uncertainty in them. The repetitions which occur stress this feeling of absolute certainty and are reminiscent of the repetitions which are often found in prayers. Celan denies the reassurances of Hölderlin's "Patmos" and of the Psalms that salvation is at hand. Some of Hölderlin's poems, "Patmos" included, refer to the darkness which descended upon the earth after the Ascension of Christ and in which man has been living ever since. "Tenebrae" confirms this view although not in the same spirit in which it was originally formulated. "Tenebrae," darkness, followed the crucifixion, but its duration was longer than the three hours of that afternoon. The entire circle of time from the beginning of the Christian era to the gas chambers of Auschwitz has been one long dark night for the Jews. The *Catholic Encyclopaedia* of 1912 reports as follows on the Catholic religious service *tenebrae*: "Lauds follows immediately on Matins, which in this occasion terminate with the close of day in order to signify the Setting of the Sun of Justice and the darkness of the Jewish people who knew not our Lord and condemned Him to the gibbet of the cross." Celan's poem responds to the anti-Semitism of which this statement is typical and describes the darkness of the Jews, from a rather different perspective.

III "Sprachgitter"

Like "Tenebrae," the title poem of the collection is a "Widerruf." It is "Sprachgitter," SG, 28.

> Augenrund zwischen den Stäben.
>
> Flimmertier Lid
> rudert nach oben,
> gibt einen Blick frei.
>
> Iris, Schwimmerin, traumlos und trüb:
> der Himmel, herzgrau, muß nah sein.
>
> Schräg, in der eisernen Tülle,
> der blakende Span.
> Am Lichtsinn
> errätst du die Seele.

> (Wär ich wie du. Wärst du wie ich.
> Standen wir nicht
> unter *einem* Passat?
> Wir sind Fremde.)
>
> Die Fliesen. Darauf,
> dicht beieinander, die beiden
> herzgrauen Lachen:
> zwei
> Mundvoll Schweigen.

(Eye, round, between the bars.//Cilia lid rows upwards, releases a glance.//Iris, swimmer, dreamless and drab: heaven, heart-gray, must be nigh.//Oblique, in the iron socket, the smoldering splinter. By the sense of light you fathom the soul.//[If I were like you. If you were like me. Did we not stand under *one* trade wind? We are strangers.]//The tiles. On them close together, the two heart-gray puddles: two mouthsful of silence.)

Two basic sources of the "Widerruf" can be cited, the one literary and the other Biblical. The literary source is the essay *Probleme der Lyrik* by Gottfried Benn, who was mentioned briefly in connection with Celan's Meridian speech.[10] Benn, in his essay, affirms his belief in the power of the word and the poem. He seeks to describe the nature of the poetic word by means of a metaphor. Referring to an essay he wrote many years earlier, he describes a kind of organism which lives in the ocean and is covered with "Flimmerhaare." These "Flimmerhaare" ("cilia") function as the sense organs of the tiny creatures; they serve to establish and define the relationship between the organisms and their environment. Benn goes on to draw his comparison in detail:

Imagine a person covered with such cilia, not only the brain but the entire being. Their function is a specific one . . . it applies to the word. . . . These cilia are not always active, [but] they have their hour. The lyrical *ich* is a fragmented *ich*, a *Gitter-ich.* . . . It always waits for its hour, in which it can become warm for an instant, it waits for its southern complex with its "seething value," its intoxication value, in which . . . the destruction of reality, which produces freedom for the poem—through words—can be effected.

The *ich*, then, must await the auspicious moment in which the proper combination of words can be found which will provide freedom for the poem. Benn continues:

Now, perhaps, words are approaching, words in confusion, not yet clear, but the cilia grope towards them. Perhaps there is an affinity for blue. . . . Think of this eternal and beautiful word! . . . It is the south-word par excellence.[11]

The primary Biblical allusion in "Sprachgitter" is to Psalm 126:1-4:

When the Lord turned again the captivity [*Gefangene*] of Zion, we were like them that dream. Then was our mouth filled with laughter [*Lachen*], and our tongue with singing: then said they among the heathen, the Lord hath done great things for them. The Lord hath done great things for us; whereof we are glad. Turn again our captivity [*Gefängnis*], O Lord, as the streams in the south. They that sow in tears shall reap in joy.[12]

The title itself, "Sprachgitter," is the first allusion to Benn's "Gitter-ich" of the essay, and it also calls to mind his poem "Die Gitter,"[13] in which "Gitter," bars, isolate the speaker from the world. A prison is suggested by the term "Gitter"; Benn's "freedom for the poem—through words" is an illusion, Celan implies. Words, and the poem, remain imprisoned, locked securely behind the bars of language. A "Widerruf" of the 126th Psalm is also implied in the prison image. The children of Israel, like language, have not been released from prison, the assurances of God and Gottfried Benn notwithstanding.

The first stanza of the poem describes an eye with the eye lashes. The power of the prison image is strengthened by the reference to the lashes as "bars." The second stanza contains another direct reference to Benn's essay; his "Flimmerhaare," which grope for words, become the "Flimmertier Lid," which is also struggling for communication.[14] This stanza also introduces water imagery, another important aspect of Benn's essay and of the "Widerruf." The combination of language, water, and an eye looking up is evocative of the final line of "Nächtlich geschürzt" (SS, 49f.), where the dead word is washed prior to the ascent of its eye. In "Sprachgitter," however, the tone is not as hopeful. The reference to rowing upwards suggests great

difficulty and hence, in spite of the apparent victory implied
in the phrase "releases a glance," the ultimate success of the
attempt to remove the bars of the prison is called into question.

The negative tone is strikingly confirmed in the third stanza.
The iris is dull and dreamless, alien to the healing world of
the dream described in "Edgar Jené und der Traum vom
Traume," and of the first verse of the Psalm. The formulation
"iris, swimmer," evokes the picture of an eye filled with tears.
Here, as throughout the poem, a powerful, yet apparently un-
emotional image conceals an intensely felt but largely subdued
complex of emotions. In addition to a part of the eye, "Iris"
suggests the Greek goddess Iris, the messenger of the gods and,
accordingly, an agent of communication. The ease and swiftness
of the goddess's movement stand in sharp contrast to the
lethargy of the iris in the poem. Iris, furthermore, is the Greek
word for rainbow, the radiantly colorful symbol of God's promise
following the deluge never to send a similar flood again. The
iris of the poem shows no similarity to the brilliant rainbow,
hence the emptiness of God's promises is suggested. The special-
ized meaning of "diffraction grating" for "Gitter" is applicable
here. Normally, light which enters the grating is filtered into
the seven colors of the rainbow. Here only gray is present;
the "Gitter" is as ineffective in its role as an order-bringing
agent as it is effective in its role as an agent of imprisonment.
The compound "herzgrau" has extremely negative connotations.
It underscores the complete grayness of the sky, reminding the
reader of the colors of the rainbow which are lacking in the
landscape of the poem. A further allusion to Benn is also present.
The "blue sky of Zanzibar" mentioned by him has turned gray;
Celan is almost systematically developing his refutation of
Benn's carefully constructed argument.

The prison image is further developed in the fourth stanza.
Its first two lines describe a smoldering piece of wood in a
niche in the wall of a dark room, such as might be found in a
prison. But again this is an image representing the condition
of the eye. The eye itself is called a "blakender Span," an object
which once provided (or which should provide) a brilliant
light, but now gives off dark smoke instead. The eye is, traditionally, the mirror of the soul. Here, too, the condition of the
soul is reflected by the "Lichtsinn" of the eye; it is the smolder-

ing remnant of something potentially brilliant. As Lyon has
observed, "Glanz" and similar words occur frequently in Celan's
poems, always as an image connected with speech.[15] The absence
of light in "Sprachgitter" is, accordingly, indicative of the
absence of communication. This use of the imagery of light
and darkness is reminiscent of a Benn poem which contains
thoughts quite similar to those expressed in the section of
Probleme der Lyrik quoted above. The poem is "Ein Wort":[16]

> Ein Wort, ein Satz—aus Chiffren steigen
> erkanntes Leben, jäher Sinn,
> die Sonne steht, die Sphären schweigen
> und alles ballt sich zu ihm hin.
>
> Ein Wort—ein Glanz, ein Flug, ein Feuer,
> ein Flammenwurf, ein Sternenstrich—
> und wieder Dunkel, ungeheuer,
> im leeren Raum um Welt und Ich.

(A word, a sentence—out of ciphers rises conscious life, sudden
meaning, the sun stands still, the spheres are silent and everything
congeals around it [the word].//A word—a flash, a flight, a fire, a
tongue of flame, a flashing star—and again darkness, terrible, in
empty space around the world and the *ich*.)

The condition described in Benn's poem is different from the
situation depicted in "Sprachgitter," where the eye's search for
the blue sky is not successful, the word is not found, the brilliance of communication is not attained.

In the fifth stanza an I-thou relationship is described. At
one time their relationship was close, or at least held the promise
of being close. But now a gulf separates them, and they are
strangers. The nature of the I and the thou is problematical,
as is often the case in Celan's poetry. They may represent two
lovers or two aspects of the poet's self. A third possibility,
implicit in the allusions to the 126th Psalm, is the poet and
the Jewish people. The word "Passat" may supply one confirmation of this hypothesis. It is an unusual word, and while it can
readily be interpreted in a meaningful way, the context by no
means demands its presence; if it merely suggests a force
bringing, or potentially bringing, the I and thou together,

numerous other images could serve as well or even better. Celan invariably selects his words with extreme care, so it would seem that a second reference must be contained in the word. The most likely one is the Jewish passover, the German word for which is "Passah." This celebration is of such central importance in Judaism that Hanna Vogt offers a description of its rituals as an introduction to her history of the Jewish people, *Joch und Krone*.[17] Vogt describes how the festival, characterized by family prayers and a strong sense of tradition, commemorates the many blessings bestowed upon the Jews by God. She concludes her description as follows: "And in this manner the Jewish people, recipients of miracles in the past, await the miracle of salvation." The thou would, then, be Judaism, from which the speaker is estranged; or, on another level, the immediate family, with which he formerly celebrated the feast and from which he is now separated by death. The "Sprachgitter" would then once again refer to the German language, which perhaps is thought to form a barrier between the speaker and the dead mother. The Jewish "Passah" becomes "Passat," which suggests the remoteness and esoteric nature of Benn's South Sea Utopia of the poetic word.

The final stanza begins with an elliptical sentence: "Die Fliesen." This construction emphasizes the importance of the tiles of the floor and indicates that the gaze of the eye, which earlier sought freedom in the heavens, is now directed downward. Its quest for freedom has met with failure. On the floor there are two "Lachen," and they are "herzgrau," the color of the sky. The primary meaning of "Lachen" in this context would be "puddles of water." Thus the water imagery is once again taken up, but all positive connotations have disappeared. Just as blue, stressed by Benn as being essential to the magical mood necessary for the creation of poetry, was absent from the sky in the third stanza, so here Benn's blue ocean is transformed into two gray puddles. The second meaning of "Lachen," "laughter," provides another reference to the 126th Psalm: "Then was our mouth filled with laughter. . . . The Lord hath done great things for us." It is no longer possible to speak of "our mouth" in the singular. There are now two mouths, which are separated, and in place of laughter they are filled with silence. The laughter ("Lachen") is instead two puddles of water, having turned into the tears mentioned in the fifth verse of the Psalm. The tears remain; joy has not been sown.

Verbal parallels to "Gespräch im Gebirg" (1959) confirm the poem's Jewish frame of reference. In his final speech, the Jew Klein reports: "Auf dem Stein bin ich gelegen, damals, du weißt, auf den Steinfliesen; und neben mir, da sind sie gelegen, die andern, die wie ich waren, die andern, die anders waren als ich und genauso, die Geschwisterkinder." ("I lay on the stone, then, you know, on the stone tiles; and next to me, there they lay, the others, who were like me, the others, who were different from, and exactly like me, the cousins.") Celan here looks back to the time of the composition of "Sprachgitter" (1957) and says that he was then separated from his fellow Jews as they lay on the tiles. Klein proceeds to mention the burning of the Sabbath candle, which thus is apparently the light mentioned in "Sprachgitter." He concludes by saying that he is moving upwards, away from the tiles, in the company of the love of the Jews, from whom he had felt estranged.

Like so many of Celan's poems, "Sprachgitter" is remarkably complex. Basically, it is a refutation of Benn's assertion that the *ich* can find words and thereby gain access to the mysteries of the blue sky and ocean. The speaker in Celan's poem feels alienated from the thou, perhaps from a beloved, and certainly from his poetry—which he writes in German—from his dead mother, and from his fellow Jews, the great majority of whom do not share his emotional reaction to the holocaust.

IV   "Allerseelen"

Celan's distance from Judaism at the time the poems of *Sprachgitter* were written has been noted by Peter Mayer.[18] The title poem clearly demonstrates the validity of Mayer's assessment, as does the poem to which he specifically refers, "Allerseelen" ("All Souls," SG, 43).

> Was hab ich
> getan?
> Die Nacht besamt, als könnt es
> noch andere geben, nächtiger als
> diese.

Vogelflug, Steinflug, tausend
beschriebene Bahnen. Blicke,
geraubt und gepflückt. Das Meer,
gekostet, vertrunken, verträumt. Eine Stunde,
seelenverfinstert. Die nächste, ein Herbstlicht,
dargebracht einem blinden
Gefühl, das des Wegs kam. Andere, viele,
ortlos und schwer aus sich selbst: erblickt und umgangen.
Findlinge, Sterne,
schwarz und voll Sprache: benannt
nach zerschwiegenem Schwur.

Und einmal (wann? auch dies ist vergessen):
den Widerhaken gefühlt,
wo der Puls den Gegentakt wagte.

(What have I done? Impregnated the night, as though there could
be others, more nocturnal than this one.//Bird flight, stone flight,
a thousand described courses. Glances, stolen and plucked. The sea,
tasted, consumed, dreamed away. An hour, soul-darkened. The next
one, an autumn light, presented to a blind feeling which came by.
Others, many, without places and heavy of themselves: seen and
avoided. Foundlings [or: glacial boulders], stars, black and full of
language: named after an oath silenced to pieces.//And once (when?
this, too, is forgotten): felt the barbed hook, when the pulse dared
the counter beat.

   The title, like that of "Tenebrae," refers to a part of the
Catholic ritual; All Souls' Day, November 2nd, is the day on
which the dead are commemorated. "Allerseelen" contains the
speaker's reflections on the Jewish dead and on his relationship
to them and to Christianity. He first asks a direct question.
There is, however, no clear-cut, direct answer and thus the
answer must be attempted in images. The image of the third
line, "impregnated the night," to describe what the speaker
has been doing, calls to mind the final section of "Stimmen,"
in which "No voice, a late-sound" is further characterized as
a "Fruchtblatt" (the part of the female reproductive system of
a plant which receives the fertilizing male "seed"). In "Stimmen"
the *Fruchtblatt* is described as having a wound which will not
heal. The implication of "Allerseelen" is similar. The abandoning
of the Jewish "voice" in the poetry has not led the poet out of
the night. On the contrary, the night has as a result been made

fertile and has accordingly "reproduced," or grown darker. The use of the subjunctive—a touch of irony—indicates that the speaker is not satisfied with the results he has achieved in impregnating the night.

The long middle stanza is filled with Celan's favorite words and images. Each is portrayed in a vaguely negative perspective, again indicating dissatisfaction. The considerable stylistic variations suggest the degree of the dissatisfaction felt by the speaker; the repeated use of the past participle emphasizes the number of instances in the past and contains the implication that what is done is done—hence the intensity of the emotion. The prefix "ver-," here suggesting that something has been wasted, is used repeatedly, and "zer-," implying destruction, appears in the final line. The first three lines of the stanza suggest the lack of success, in general terms. The next image, "an hour, soul-darkened," refers back to the title and also suggests the darkness encountered in the poem "Tenebrae." The only light present is the "autumn light." Autumn, it will be recalled, is one of the words of Celan's early poetry which is most intimately associated with the poet's personal experiences. It appears in eight of the poems in *Mohn und Gedächtnis* (seven of these occur before "Todesfuge"), in only two poems in *Von Schwelle zu Schwelle,* and only this one time in *Sprachgitter.* The disappearance of the word "Herbst" dramatically illustrates the sharp decrease in the use of a personal idiom as the poetry develops. This is one aspect of what the speaker "has done," and the reintroduction of "autumn" into the poetry alludes to his awareness of this aspect of the problem. Many "others"— that is, other emotional encounters with some aspect of the Jewish past—have followed; they are avoided and are, accordingly, described here in vague terms.

That the images actually relate to Judaism is confirmed by the final lines of the stanza where they are called "stars." They are also called "Findlinge," a word which means both "found-ling"—suggesting the poet's broken relationship to Judaism—and "erratic" boulder, that is, a rock which has been displaced by glacial action. Celan here alludes to the icy landscape inhabited by the Jews, and by himself, which recurs in his works from the early "Schwarze Flocken" and the Jené essay to the late poetry. The images represent the dark, unspoken words impris-

oned within the "Sprachgitter." The final phrase is ambiguous.
as is its English equivalent: "named after an oath silenced to
pieces." The preposition "nach" ("after") can carry temporal
connotations as well as the more natural idiomatic meaning
inherent in the phrase "to be named after someone." The emotion
is further intensified in the final stanza through the use of two
prefixes suggesting resistance or opposition, "wider-" and
"gegen-." The first line of the stanza is best interpreted as an
indication that the attempts to counter the trend in the past
were infrequent and without consequence, and not that there
has been a single attempt which the speaker has forgotten.

CHAPTER 6

Die Niemandsrose

I *The Return to Judaism*

AS MANY, but by no means all, of the reviewers observed, *Die Niemandsrose* (1963) marks a return to Judaism. The book contains Celan's second and final dedication, "To the Memory of Osip Mandelshtam," the Russian Jewish poet who was exiled and killed in the Stalinist Russia of the late 1930's, and who is, accordingly, a representative of the Jewish victims of all ages.[1] The opening poem of the collection confirms the Jewish theme of the book and clearly demonstrates that, for Celan, the realities of the concentration camps are still as vividly present as they were in 1945 when "Todesfuge" was written. This poem is called "Es war Erde in ihnen" (NR, 9).

Es war Erde in ihnen, und
sie gruben.

Sie gruben und gruben, so ging
ihr Tag dahin, ihre Nacht. Und sie lobten nicht Gott,
der, so hörten sie, alles dies wollte,
der, so hörten sie, alles dies wußte.

Sie gruben und hörten nichts mehr;
sie wurden nicht weise, erfanden kein Lied,
erdachten sich keinerlei Sprache.
Sie gruben.

Es kam eine Stille, es kam auch ein Sturm,
es kamen die Meere alle.
Ich grabe, du gräbst, und es gräbt auch der Wurm,
und das Singende dort sagt: Sie graben.

O einer, o keiner, o niemand, o du:
Wohin gings, da's nirgendhin ging?

O du gräbst und ich grab, und ich grab mich dir zu,
und am Finger erwacht uns der Ring.

(There was earth in them and they dug.//They dug and they dug,
in this manner their day passed, their night. And they did not praise
God, who, so they heard, wanted all this, who, so they heard, knew
all this.//They dug and heard nothing else; they did not become
wise, invented no song, thought up no kind of language. They dug.//
There came a calm, there came also a storm, there came the seas
one and all. I dig, you dig and the worm digs too, and that which
is singing there says: they are digging.// O one, O none, O no-one,
O thou: where did it lead, when it led nowhere? O you dig and
I dig and I dig through to you, and our rings awaken on our fingers.)

The opening stanza is an unmistakable allusion to, and
reaffirmation of, the enduring validity of "Todesfuge."[2] "Erde"
and "gruben" immediately call to mind "Erde," "Erdreich," and
"schaufeln ein Grab" from the earlier poem. The second stanza
strengthens the allusion to "Todesfuge"; the repetition "sie
gruben und gruben" is reminiscent of the repetitions "wir trinken
und trinken," and the phrase "ihr Tag ... ihre Nacht" calls to
mind the similar passing of time in "Todesfuge": "morgens und
mittags und nachts." The reaction of the Jews to the situation,
left implicit—and accordingly open to misinterpretation—in the
earlier poem is explicitly stated here: "they did not praise God."
The abrupt change within the fourth line from "day and night"
to "And they did not praise God" stresses the close relationship
between the two factors. The enjambment between lines three
and four, in conjunction with the apparently strong stop between
"Night" and "And," gives emphasis to the continuity of thought.
The last two lines of the second stanza directly reflect the attitude
repeatedly expressed by writers such as Richard Rubenstein, who
has said:

How can Jews believe in an omnipotent, beneficent God after
Auschwitz? Traditional Jewish theology ... has interpreted every
major catastrophe in Jewish history as God's punishment of a sinful
Israel. I fail to see how this position can be maintained without
regarding Hitler and the SS as instruments of God's will.[3]

The third stanza and the first half of the fourth use images
to describe the condition of the Jews during the holocaust. In the

last two lines of the fourth stanza the perspective shifts. The third person plural which has been used previously, suggesting the impersonal nature of the camps and their victims, changes to I and thou, again reminiscent of "Todesfuge," where the pronoun applied to the black milk shifts from "it" to "thou." The "Wurm" (a word which has a broader range of meaning than the English "worm") is still another example of a comparison between Jews and animals in Celan. The tense here changes from past to present. This suggests the lingering effects of the holocaust for the living as well as for the dead. It also indicates that the I and the thou now share the same activity; they are growing closer together. The first line of the final stanza refers to the Jewish people who are "one," "united in their fate," but "no one" and "none," because they have been largely exterminated. The first line of the final stanza contains the word "niemand," which is present in the title of the collection. Sometimes, as in "Psalm," it is applied to God. In this poem, it refers to the dead Jews who have been systematically killed and, hence, are "no one."

It remains unspecified to whom the question asked in the second line of the last stanza is addressed. On one level it refers to the Jews, whose digging leads "nirgendhin," nowhere and into nothingness, i.e., death. But in light of the final two lines and of Celan's continual search for identity it also would seem to refer to the poet and his attempt, in *Von Schwelle zu Schwelle* and *Sprachgitter*—roughly 1948 to 1959—to leave behind the traditions of his Jewish heritage. The combined efforts are now at last beginning to be productive: "I dig through to you." After a long separation and much effort the *ich* finally succeeds in establishing contact with the *du*. The final line alludes to the ring, which symbolizes fidelity. The passage from the Jené essay, "To whom did we swear fidelity," is called to mind, as are the rusty rings of "Ein lied in der Wüste" (MG, 9). At last the bond between Celan and his Jewish past seems to have been reestablished.

In his review of *Die Niemandsrose* Beda Allemann writes: "Celan sometimes steps forward in this volume with the almost naive attitude of someone just freed."[4] This is an apt description of the mood prevailing in many of the poems. The sense of freedom and release felt in the poems can be clearly seen in "Es war Erde in ihnen." It does not come from any attitude or feeling of reconciliation with God or Germans or Christians, but rather from an expressed awareness of having accepted Judaism in all its aspects. Some of the stylistic traits of the poems of *Mohn und Gedächtnis* reappear in *Die Niemandsrose*. Rhyme, for example, is used on occasion, although usually for a specific, unusual effect; the lines are, on the average, longer than those in *Sprachgitter* and the rhythm is often close to that which is characteristic of the early poems. Lines consisting of a single word are, to be sure, not uncommon; but now they tend to be concentrated in certain poems, again for a specific, unusual effect.[5]

In other ways, too, the book continues in the direction indicated in *Sprachgitter;* for example, the four cycles all lack titles, and fragmentation, suggested especially by such configurations as "... Ver-/ schwisterte, Zu-/ geschleuderte, du" (an approximation might be: "... sis-/ terly, cat-/ apulted, thou") is much in evidence. The stylistic traits of a small number of poems, most noticeably "Anabasis" (NR, 54), definitely point forward to *Atemwende* (1967); many poems contain hints of a movement in this direction. The most prominent of these traits is constituted by apparent nonsense words and other totally enigmatic words and constructions. But the most significant aspect of *Die Niemandsrose* is its conscious Jewishness, and my analysis will largely consist in a discussion of Judaic themes and references in certain key poems.

The poem "Zürich, zum Storchen" (NR, 12f.; "zum Storchen" is a hotel in Zurich) is dedicated to Nelly Sachs, a Jewish poetess who barely managed to escape from Nazi Germany in 1940. The identity of the thou of the poem is accordingly clear in this particular case. The poem describes a conversation between the two poets which revolved around Jewish subjects. Among other topics, "Von deinem Gott war die Rede, ich sprach/ gegen ihn, ..." ("There was talk about your God; I spoke against him"). The first implication in these words is similar to that of the lines from "Es war Erde in ihnen," "And they did not praise God, ... who wanted all this." Nelly Sachs's attitude toward the holocaust is also called into question. Olof Lagercrantz summarizes the attitudes of the poetess as follows: "The Bible teaches her to see something universal and representative in the deaths of the Jews.... They are the suffering people, and as such they represent all peoples, the German as well as the Jewish...."[6] This

accurately expresses her sentiments—insofar as such generaliza-
tions can be valid. These are, however, not the sentiments of
certain other Jews, Paul Celan, for example, as reflected indirectly
in his poetry, or Elie Wiesel, as openly expressed throughout his
writings.

Siegbert Prawer explains the title of the poem "Zwölf Jahre"
(NR, 18) as a reference to the "twelve years" of Nazi rule in
Germany (1933-1945).[7] Peter Mayer explains it on the basis of
an allusion in the first stanza of the poem:[8]

> Die wahr—
> gebliebene, wahr—
> gewordene Zeile: . . . *dein*
> *Haus in Paris—zur*
> *Opferstatt deiner Hände.*

(This line which has remained true, which has become true: *your
house in Paris—your hands' place of sacrifice.*)

The italicized words were emphasized by Celan because they
are a direct quotation from "Auf Reisen" (MG, 43), the poem
immediately following "Todesfuge" in *Mohn und Gedächtnis*.
The twelve years refer to the time elapsing between Celan's
move to Paris (1948) and the present (approximately 1960).
Celan did not live in Paris when the poem was written, and its
position following "Todesfuge" imparts to it the suggestion of
a new beginning, a move away from the holocaust, geographical-
ly, intellectually, and emotionally. But the words, which com-
prised a single long line in the original poem, are now fragmented, suggesting the failure of the attempt. The thought
expressed in the line has remained true in one sense and become
true in another sense: the house in Paris was no panacea. The
second stanza runs:

> Dreimal durchatmet,
> dreimal durchglänzt.

(Three times breathed through, three times shined through.)

They suggest, perhaps, a third period of twelve years in the
poet's life, from his birth late in 1920 to the beginning of
Hitler's Third Reich early in 1933. This stanza is followed by

a line consisting solely of dots, and a very somber third stanza:
"...I see poison blooming...." The final stanza suggests a
change of direction: "Geh. Komm./ Die Liebe löscht ihren
Namen: sie/ schreibt sich dir zu" ("Go. Come. Love extinguishes
their names. It assigns itself to you"). "Go" away from the old;
"come" back to your Judaic heritage—begin a new era in your
life—this is how the speaker admonishes himself. The poem
probably reflects an autobiographical situation. Milo Dor reports
that after the publication of *Sprachgitter* Celan came to Vienna
—which was as close to his native land and culture as he could
have hoped to get—and investigated the possibilities of settling
there permanently. But nothing came of the attempt, apparently
because Celan could not find a suitable means of earning a
living in Vienna.[9]

The references to Judaism in "Die Schleuse" ("The Locks,"
NR, 20), are quite direct; the final stanzas run: "An/die Viel-
götterei/ verlor ich ein Wort, das mich suchte:/ *Kaddisch.*//
Durch/ die Schleuse mußt ich,/ das Wort in die Salzflut zurück-/
und hinaus- und hinüberzuretten:/ *Jiskor*" ("To polytheism I
lost a word which was seeking me: *Kaddish.*// I was forced to
go through the [canal] locks to save the word back to and
beyond and over into the salt-flood: *Jiskor*"). Both italicized
words are Jewish prayers relating to the remembrance of the
dead. The speaker has sought them and been sought by them,
as in "Es war Erde in ihnen." The emphasis is on ritual and
tradition, however, and not on actual religious belief. Devotion
to such matters of form and ritual even by non-believing Jews
is quite common.

The references in "Stumme Herbstgerüche" ("Silent Autumn
Scents," NR, 21) are much more veiled and personal, and are
most readily interpreted following an examination of a few key
words in "Radix, matrix" (NR, 37f.), a very complicated poem
which is built around numerous references.[10] The third and
fourth stanzas of this poem establish the Jewish frame of reference: "Wer,/ wer wars, jenes/ Geschlecht, jenes gemordete,
jenes/ schwarz in den Himmel stehende:/ Rute und Hode—?//
(Wurzel/ Wurzel Abrahams. Wurzel Jesse. Niemandes/ Wurzel
—o/ unser.") ("Who, who was it, that race [or: "sex"], that
murdered race, standing black into the sky, penis [or: "rod"]
and testicle—? Root. Root of Abraham. Root of Jesse. No one's

root—O ours.") The origin of this image can be found in Isaiah
11, a prophecy of the coming of the Messiah: "And there shall
come forth a rod [*Rute*] out of the stem of Jesse, and a Branch
shall grow out of his roots [Wurzel]" (11:1; cf. also 11:11).

The poem addresses a thou, which Weissenberger identifies
as the dead mother, an extension of the "matrix" of the title:
"Wie man zum Stein spricht, wie/ du,/ mir vom Abgrund her,
von/ einer Heimat her ver-/ schwisterte, Zu-/ geschleuderte,
du,/ du mir vorzeiten...// Damals, da ich nicht da war,..."
("As one speaks to the stone, as you, related to me, catapulted
to me from one home, from the abyss, you who, for me, before
time began,....") Weissenberger offers the following explanation of the meaning of these puzzling lines: "The motherly thou
was 'related like a sister' to the speaker in the stage before birth,
in 'abyss' and 'home.' "

Similar language occurs in "Stumme Herbstgerüche":

> Stumme Herbstgerüche. Die
> Sternblume, ungeknickt, ging
> zwischen Heimat und Abgrund durch
> dein Gedächtnis.
>
> Eine fremde Verlorenheit war
> gestalthaft zugegen, du hättest
> beinah
> gelebt.

(Silent autumn scents. The star-flower, unplucked, went between
home and abyss through your memory.//A strange sense of loss was
present like a figure, as though you almost lived.)

"Herbst," one of the most personal and intimate words in
Celan's vocabulary, strongly suggests the past, specifically the
relationship between the speaker and the mother. The "Sternblume" is, in essence, a synonym for "Niemandsrose," since both
the star and the rose suggest the Jews. The combination of
"home" and "abyss" suggests, as in "Radix, matrix," the time
before the holocaust; perhaps childhood is recalled in the present poem, the time when the "Sternblume" was still intact, "unplucked." The second stanza is vague and the *du* probably
embodies both the speaker and the mother. His experiencing of

a strange sense of loss in recalling the past then leads, in turn, to the ambiguous statement, "you almost lived." What he is saying here is that, in a sense, his life has never begun, because of the holocaust, just as surely as his mother's life ended then, while implying that both came close, in some unspecified manner, to surviving.

The long title of the final poem of the first cycle includes some Jewish references: "Eine Gauner- und Ganovenweise gesungen zu Paris emprès pontoise von Paul Celan aus Czernowitz bei Sadagora" ("A Swindler and Rascal Song Sung in Paris emprès pontoise by Paul Celan from Czernowitz near Sadagora," NR, 27f.). The final phrase in the title is unusual since Czernowitz is by far the larger city. The emphasis is placed upon Sadagora because, as Meinecke and Peter Mayer have noted, this small town was a major center of Hassidism.[11] The motto affixed to the poem is the most direct statement of anti-Christian feeling to be found in all of Celan's poetry—and even that is veiled. It is: "'Manchmal nur, in dunklen Zeiten' Heinrich Heine, An Edom." ("Only sometimes, in dark times"; Edom refers to the enemies of the Jews). The first two stanzas of "An Edom," a poem by Heinrich Heine (1797-1856), run: "For a thousand years now, and longer, we have been tolerating each other like brothers. You, you tolerate my breathing, and I tolerate your raging. Only sometimes, in dark times, your attitude changed and you colored your loving, pious paws with my blood." Paul Celan, like Heine a Jew living in exile in Paris, like Heine sings his song to the enemies of the Jews. Celan's poem contains numerous additional references to Judaism, including the word "Mandelbaum" ("almond tree"), an obvious allusion to Osip Mandelshtam.

"Zweihäusig, Ewiger" (NR, 45) is one of Celan's most irreverent poems. The first word in the title, literally "two-housed," refers to bisexual forms of life capable of reproduction without benefit of external fertilization. The second word, "Eternal One," refers unambiguously to God. The house image is further developed in the poem, as is the sexual imagery. God is described as "uninhabitable," and therefore the I and thou must build their own place for sleeping. This place stands in the rain, which is a common metaphor for the grace of God. The poem continues:

> . . . Er
> hat dann genug an sich selber, zweimal.
>
> Laß ihn, er
> habe sich ganz, als das Halbe
> und abermals Halbe. Wir,
> wir sind das Regenbett, er
> komme und lege uns trocken.
>
> . . . .
>
> Er kommt nicht, er legt uns nicht trocken.

(He is then satisfied with himself, twice. Let him, he has, himself, completely, as the half and once again half. We, we are the rain-bed, let him come and dry us out [or: change our diapers]. . . . He won't come, he won't dry us out [or: change our diapers].)

The first four lines quoted above refer to the Christian account of the Trinity; God "reproduced" himself twice or "halved" himself twice. The speaker and the thou are wet from the rain of God's grace, and the request made to God that he should come and "change their diapers" is a fitting climax to a blasphemous poem describing God's lack of attention to his children. The speaker declares his love for the beloved, for the Jewish people and its traditions, even though the love will have to flourish without the benefit of God's help. Again, a statement by Richard Rubenstein comes to mind: "We stand in a cold, silent, unfeeling cosmos, unaided by any purposeful power beyond our own resources. After Auschwitz, what else can a Jew say about God?"[12]

A more abstract poem is "Ein Wurfholz" (NR, 56). The "Wurfholz" is a boomerang which "wanders on breath-roads."[13] In the exact center of the poem, corresponding to the farthest reach of the flight of the boomerang, is the line "sich selber der Reim" ("the rhyme itself"), a line which actually constitutes the first half of a rhyme pair. The following lines are: "so kommt es/ geflogen, so kommts/ wieder und heim" ("so it comes flying, so it comes, again and home"). The rhyme of the final couplet of the early poem "Nähe der Gräber," "Reim—heim," is repeated, indicating the return of the voice of the Jewish poet. As Peter Mayer says, "That which was apparently

mis-thrown returns to its origins in destruction, encounters itself there, is itself 'the rhyme.' "

A very difficult and equally significant poem is "Hinausgekrönt" ("Crowned outward," NR, 69f.). The second stanza
establishes a tenuous relationship with Celan's early works by
means of an allusion to stars and the hair of Berenice: "Bei
welchen/ Sternen! Lauter/ graugeschlagenes Herzhammersilber.
Und/ Berenikes Haupthaar, auch hier,—ich flocht,/ ich zer-
flocht,/ ich flechte, zerflechte...." ("By what stars! Nothing
but gray-beaten heart-hammer-silver. And Berenice's hair, here
too—I braided, and braided to pieces, I braid and braid to
pieces"). The phrase "here too" establishes a link with a previous
work, "Edgar Jené und der Traum vom Traume," where this
unusual constellation is also mentioned. The change from past
to present tense seems to indicate that the relationship between
the *ich* and the constellation is the same now as it was in the
past when it was first established, or recognized. I suggested
above that the constellation suggests the beginning of the down-
fall of the Jewish people. The importance of a second implication can now be seen; the hair was originally dedicated to
Aphrodite. Thus an erotic element is suggested, once again
occasioning the association of the Jewish people with an erotic
image. The third stanza refers to a "beloved," and explicit sexual imagery appears in the fourth stanza. The fifth stanza
explains, to some extent, the complicated relationships: "Mit
Namen, getränkt/ von jedem Exil./ Mit Namen und Samen,/
mit Namen, getaucht/ in alle/ Kelche, die vollstehn mit deinem/
Königsblut, Mensch,—in alle/ Kelche der großen/ Ghetto-Rose,
aus der/ du uns ansiehst, unsterblich von soviel/ auf Morgen-
wegen gestorbenen Toden." ("With names, steeped in every
exile. With names and seed, with names immersed in all the
chalices filled with your kingly blood, o man, in all calyxes of
the great ghetto-rose, from which you look at us, made immortal
by so many deaths died on morning paths.") The many periods
of exile which the Jews have lived through are mentioned here.
The word play "Namen—Samen" ("name—seed") suggests the
function of the sexual imagery, as in other poems where such
images occur as "... Die Nacht besamt" ("fertilized the night,"
SG, 43). The names are dipped in the chalices which are full
of "your kingly blood, o man." This is an allusion to Christ, whose

kingly blood filled the chalice at the Last Supper. But it is a bitter and ironic allusion, since only if he were God could the wine in the chalice have been turned into blood, and here he is specifically called "man, human being." As the result of a play on two meanings of "Kelch," the Christian chalice becomes the calyx of the Jewish rose. The rose is characterized as the "Ghettorose," since Christianity was responsible for the creation of the Ghettos.[14] Passages in such poems as "Hinausgekrönt," "Spät und tief," and "Tenebrae" strongly indicate that Celan would have agreed with theologians like Richard Rubenstein in assigning the roots of the death camps to Christian philosophy.

In concluding I will briefly mention three long, complicated poems near the end of Die Niemandsrose which have the poet's Judaism as their theme. As Dietlind Meinecke—who rarely mentions the Judaic aspect of Celan's poetry—observes, in "Hüttenfenster" ("Hut-Window," NR, 76f.), "Celan gives direct expression to his Judaism."[15] The theme of "Todesfuge" is once again taken up in this poem: " . . . die/ Schwebenden, die/ Menschenund-Juden,/ das Volk-vom-Gewölk," ("the hovering ones, the humans-and-Jews, the people-of-clouds,"). The word "Jude" is here contrasted, and at the same time linked, with the word "Mensch." They are literally the people of the air and the clouds, since that is where so many of them have dwelt since being murdered and cremated. The final two lines of the first stanza, "du kommst, du kommst,/ wohnen werden wir, wohnen, . . ." can be explained by a remark of Hermann Hakel. When I asked Hakel at the beginning of the interview—naively and merely in order to initiate the conversation—"Wo wohnen Sie?" ("where do you live?"), he replied that after a person has been in a concentration camp he becomes incapable of "wohnen," of living, in the sense of having a home. The attitude towards life and the consciousness of the implications of words are equally interesting, and equally applicable to Celan.

The penultimate poem of the book, "Und mit dem Buch aus Tarussa" ("And with the book from Tarussa," NR, 85) has a quotation in Russian from Marina Tsvetaeva as a motto: "All poets are Jews." The source, as well as the precise implication of the words in their original context, has not been determined. In the context of Die Niemandsrose it would seem to mean that all poets have suffered, as all Jews have suffered. The final poem,

"In der Luft" ("In the Air," NR, 88f.) is much more direct, as
the first stanza and the first three lines of the second will demonstrate: "In der Luft, da bleibt deine Wurzel, da,/ in der Luft./
Wo sich das Irdische ballt, erdig,/ Atem-und-Lehm.// Groß/
geht der Verbannte dort oben, der/ Verbrannte:" ("In the air,
there your root remains, there, in the air. Where the earthly
congeals, earthly, breath-and-clay.// Large, the exiled one goes
up there above, the cremated one.") The Jews in exile are
equated with the remnants of the cremated Jews which remain
in the air. The opening of the third stanza is extremely significant: "Mit ihm/ wandern die Meridiane: . . ."[16] The reference
to Celan's Meridian speech could not be more obvious: "Ich
finde etwas—wie die Sprache—Immaterielles, aber Irdisches,
Terrestrisches, etwas Kreisförmiges . . . ich finde . . . einen *Meridian*" (Mer, 87). The exact significance of the allusion to the
Meridian speech is not clear, however. Surely there is some irony
involved. The meridians probably correspond to, and represent,
the moods and the state of mind, or consciousness—the conception of reality—of the speaker. He finds reality on no "map
of the world" (Mer, 87), but rather in the air, with the "Atem
und Lehm"—the breath and earthly remains—of his dead mother,
and of all the Jews.

II "Psalm"

The poem from which the title of the collection is taken is
"Psalm" (NR, 23):

> Niemand knetet uns wieder aus Erde und Lehm,
> niemand bespricht unsern Staub.
> Niemand.
>
> Gelobt seist du, Niemand.
> Dir zulieb wollen
> wir blühn.
> Dir
> entgegen.
>
> Ein nichts
> waren wir, sind wir, werden
> wir bleiben, blühend:

die Nichts-, die
Niemandsrose.

Mit
dem Griffel seelenhell,
dem Staubfaden himmelswüst,
der Krone rot
vom Purpurwort, das wir sangen
über, o über
dem Dorn.

(No one will form us again out of earth and clay, no one utters
words over our dust. No one.//Praise be to thee, No-one. To please
you we want to bloom, to spite you [or: for your sake].// A nothing
were we, are we, and will we be, blooming, the nothing-rose, the
No-one's-rose.//With the pistil soul-bright, the filament heaven-
dreary, the crown red from the crimson word, which we sang, over,
oh over the thorn.)

There have been several detailed interpretations of this extraordinarily complex poem. All find a real or potential blasphemy
to be inherent in the first two stanzas. On one level, these lines
in some way deny, or seem to deny, God's power to create, his
claim to the title "creator."[17] The great majority of interpreters,
however, feel that the blasphemy is only apparent, and that
Celan is here following the old Jewish law that the name of
God must not be spoken, but rather a circumlocution must be
found. The circumlocution would, in this case, be "Niemand,"
"No-one," and hence Celan is actually affirming the God of
Judaism.[18]

"Psalm" surely contains numerous references to concepts
taken from Jewish mysticism, as well as to the Bible. But they
all seem to be distorted in some way, and I would consider them
to be, for the most part, ironic. "Psalm," then, has much in common with the usual Celan "Widerruf." The title itself is, of course,
familiar. The word "psalm" comes from a root meaning "to sing
a song of praise." The "we" of Celan's poem is, at least on one
level, the Jewish dead, singing their song of praise. Thus the
following passage from the end of the 115th and beginning of
the 116th Psalms constitutes a principal element of the Widerruf": "The dead praise not the Lord, neither any that go down
into silence. But we will bless the Lord from this time forth and

for evermore. Praise the Lord. I love the Lord because he hath
heard my voice and my supplications."

The irony and the bitterness inherent in Celan's poem, with
its allusion to this Biblical passage, seem patent. As so often, a
Biblical passage alluded to in Celan's poetry contains a statement like "the Lord . . . hath heard my voice and my supplications." The Lord did not hear the supplications of the Jews at
Auschwitz; hence the validity of the entire passage is called into
question by the poetic "Widerruf." The Psalm says that the dead
cannot praise God, but God has heard our supplications and,
therefore, we will praise him eternally. In "Psalm," the dead
praise No-one, thereby blaspheming God, because he has not
heard their supplications. By establishing "Niemand" as God,
the dead are furthermore setting up false gods, and also rejecting the statment of the Psalms that they cannot praise God; they
are in fact doing so, even if the identity of the god is different.

The complexities of the poem become apparent when the first
stanza is examined. The "We" refers first of all to the dead. But
it can also be interpreted as a reference to all Jews, living and
dead. The centuries of persecution have formed a bond which
eternally unites them, as is the case in "Es war Erde in ihnen,"
interpreted above. Another, more specific reference here is to
the German-speaking Jewish community, especially that of the
more easterly regions of Europe. This community, in which
Celan grew up and to which he feels a renewed spirit of kinship,
is dead and will never return, any more than the dead will be
reborn. Hermann Hakel also emphasizes the irretrievable loss
of the European Jewish community: "We, Celan, myself, or whoever, were born before Hitler . . . [That culture] will never exist
again, no matter how many Jews return. It is gone and will never
exist again. Never." The speaker in the poem laments this fact,
but, as he says in the following stanzas, he intends to preserve
the memory as best he can.

The Biblical reference is equally complex. To be sure, its
meaning is rather simple on one level: the speakers, the Jewish
dead, lament that "no one, no one will be able to give them
life again, No-one." In the second line, "no one" is not capitalized, which indicates that it is used in its normal sense without special connotations. The third line, consisting of the single
word, "Niemand," is an independent sentence and, accordingly,

the word must be capitalized. In the fourth line, however, "Nie-mand" is capitalized, suggesting the equation of this "No-one" with God.[19] The speakers reflect on their original statement and then reject it; they demand life; if God is absent, as the first two lines indicate, they will deify "Niemand," who has assumed the role of creator. Some implications of the vocabulary are suc-cintly summarized by William Rey: "It is significant that Celan has replaced the Biblical motif of the infusion of the living breath by the conjuration [*Besprechen*] of the dust. The emphasis falls here on the divine word rather than on the divine spirit."[20] The reference to regeneration is given in terms of the New, not the Old Testament. Allusion is again made to the ascendancy of Christianity, and the strength of the reference is enhanced by the presence within it of an allusion to the resurrection of Christ and of all men at the Last Judgment, which is primarily a Christian conception.

The first line of the second sanza contains another reference to the Psalms. The standard phrase, in Luther's translation, for "Praise be to the Lord," common in the Psalms, is "Gelobt sei der Herr." Celan has made two changes. First, the Lord is called no one, and second, the Biblical third person, "der Herr," be-comes the more intimate second person, "du, Niemand." The Jews now feel closer to "Niemand" than they ever did to their Lord. The expression "Gelobt seist du, Niemand" is an affirma-tion of absurdity and as such calls to mind Celan's Meridian speech. In discussing *Dantons Tod*, Büchner's drama about the French Revolution, Celan stressed the significance of a line spoken near the end of the drama by Lucile, who has come to see the absolute absurdity of the revolution, as well as of every-thing else in life. In a public place for all the world to hear, she screams: "Long live the king"—not because she is in favor of the restoration of the monarchy, far from it. As Celan says, offering his own interpretation: "Es ist das Gegenwort, es ist das Wort, das den 'Draht' zerreißt, ... es ist ein Akt der Freiheit. ... Gehuldigt wird hier der für die Gegenwart des Menschlichen zeugenden Majestät des Absurden" ("It is the counter-word, the word which severs the 'string' [upon which men, like puppets, are usually manipulated by outside forces], it is an act of freedom. ... What is acknowledged here is the majesty of the Absurd, which gives testimony to the presence of mankind" (Mer, 76). Celan's

"Praise be to thee, No-one," like Lucile's "Long live the king," is the most absurd thing the speaker could find to express the absurdity of life.

The rose is often used as the symbol of Israel, and one of the numerous Biblical references to this symbolism forms another basis for the extended Biblical "Widerruf" present in the poem. Ecclesiasticus 39:17f. contains the following lines: "Hearken unto me, ye holy children, and bud forth as a rose growing by the brook. . . . And sing a song of praise, bless the Lord in all his works. . . . All the works of the Lord are exceeding good." The usual elements of the "Widerruf" are present; the Biblical passage contains a reference to the goodness of God as well as vocabulary and imagery (the rose, the song of praise) similar to that of the poem in question. The second stanza of "Psalm" contains the apparently contradictory statements "We want to bloom for your sake [*dir zulieb*] and in opposition to you [*dir entgegen*]." Although it would be wrong in this, as in any particular instance, to limit the implications of Celan's paradoxical images, these two phrases probably refer to the two different figures implicit in "Niemand" and "niemand"; for the sake and glorification of absurdity, and in opposition to God, the Jews along with their traditions have flourished, are flourishing (as, for example, in Celan's poetry), and will continue to do so, as the "Nichts-, die Niemandsrose," the flower of nothingness. The phrase "dir entgegen" could also mean simply "toward you"; as often, the blasphemy is concealed in an ambiguous expression.

The final, extraordinarily complex stanza introduces imagery relating to the reproductory system of the flower, to Christ's death, to Jewish mysticism, and to Celan's role in propagating the heritage of Judaism. "Griffel" can refer either to a writing instrument or to the pistil of a flower; "Staubfaden" means specifically the filament of a flower, but must also be thought of as a compound of "Staub"—the dust of the second line of the poem—and "Faden," a thread; and "Krone" can likewise refer to a specific part of a flower. "Seelenhell" and "himmelswüst" each combine a spiritual reference with a descriptive modifier: soul and heaven, and bright and dreary, respectively. The logical frame of reference—insofar as one can speak at all of such a frame in the poem—has been lost completely. The speaker is overwhelmed by the ramifications of the emotional complex

which he is now rendering into images. Nonetheless it seems
clear that the two unusual compounds suggest the emptiness
of heaven and the brightness of the (Jewish) souls. The association of the masculine, fertilizing "Staubfaden" with the emptiness
of heaven is evocative of the inability of heaven to impregnate
the dust and revitalize the dead Jews.

The Word, which is impotent, is directly mentioned in the next
image of the last stanza: the "crown, red from the crimson word."
Schwarz briefly alludes to the connection between this passage
and the one in which the "Ghetto-Rose" appeared (i.e., to the
relationship between Judaism and Christianity), and Kostal
points out the allusion in the final four lines to Christ's crown of
thorns: ". . . crimson is not only the color of the cloak of Christ
the King, but is also the color of the blood which he—according
to Christian belief—shed for us (cf. the poem "Tenebrae," interpreted by Götz Wienold)."[21] But Kostal does not proceed to draw
what I feel are the necessary conclusions. If there is a reference
here to the blood of Christ, and a veiled allusion to, or at least
a parallel with, "Tenebrae," how can any affirmation or hope
remain, in the traditional sense? The "Widerruf" in "Psalm"
is no longer relatively simple as it was in "Corona" or "Tenebrae." The relationship between the images and the emotions
behind them is much more complex. Christ offers no hope, nor
do the affirmative aspects of Jewish mysticism to which allusion
is made, especially in the last stanza.[22] And yet, Christ himself
did not persecute the Jews, and the medieval mystics cannot be
blamed for not sharing insights into the nature of God and the
world gleaned from years of living with the "Master from Germany." Furthermore, both Jesus and the mystics were examples of
a form of the flourishing Judaic culture which the speaker desires to preserve. The ich is accordingly faced with a totally
absurd situation and his answers here, the only possible response
under the circumstances, if he is to retain his freedom, is a hymn
of praise to God and absurdity, who are one. Such an attitude
is not without historical precedent. Elie Wiesel tells of how an
inmate of the camp who had completely lost his faith requested
that Kaddish be said for him after his death. Wiesel relates that
when he asked why, the man "took the tone he always used when
he explained a passage in the Talmud to me: 'You do not see
the heart of the matter. Here and now, the only way to accuse

him is by praising him.' And he went, laughing, to his death."[23]

The degree to which the meaning of the images can be defined and limited decreases as the poem progresses, and the significance of "das wir sangen/ über, o über/ dem Dorn" cannot be stated discursively. The tense of "sangen," however, seems to give a clue regarding the function of the lines within the economy of the poem. The time suggested by the remaining verbs in the poem is, throughout, indefinite. Even the successive use of past, present, and future tenses in the third stanza strongly suggests a continuum rather than a separation between the three temporal divisions. The complex of associations suggested in the final stanza, on the other hand, were *in the past* sung "over the thorn," above the suffering of the ghettos of the earlier ages. But that time is gone. Only a psalm of praise to the absurdity of existence is now appropriate, and the most appropriate voice for such a psalm is the Jewish people, announcing their refusal to die.

III "Mandorla"

Probably the most pronounced, if not necessarily the most obvious, attack against Christianity in Celan's poetry is made in the poem "Mandorla" (NR, 42).[24]

> In der Mandel—was steht in der Mandel?
> Das Nichts.
> Es steht das Nichts in der Mandel.
> Da steht es und steht.
>
> Im Nichts—wer steht da? Der König.
> Da steht der König, der König.
> Da steht er und steht.
>
> Judenlocke, wirst nicht grau.
>
> Und dein Aug—wohin steht dein Auge?
> Dein Aug steht der Mandel entgegen.
> Dein Aug, dem Nichts stehts entgegen.
> Es steht zum König.
> So steht es und steht.
>
> Menschenlocke, wirst nicht grau.
> Leere Mandel, königsblau.

(In the almond, what is standing in the almond? Nothingness.
Nothingness is standing in the almond. There it stands and stands.//
In the Nothingness—who is standing there? The king. There stands
the king, the king. There he stands and stands//Jewish hair, you
don't get gray.// And your eye, whither is your eye directed? Your
eye is directed toward the almond. Your eye, it is directed toward
the Nothingness. It supports the king. That's how it stands and
stands.//Human hair, you don't get gray. Empty almond, royal blue.)

In the first two stanzas, the speaker describes a Mandorla—
an oval medieval picture—which formerly contained a likeness
of Jesus but is now blank. One critic recently linked the poem
with a specific picture from which the Christ-figure has been
eradicated by the elements.[25] The sight of the picture and the
verbal associations of the word "Mandorla" initiate several lines
of thought. The halo, of course, remains a halo, with its spiritual
connotations, throughout the poem. But immediately following
the first appearance of the word "Mandel" there is a dash,
indicating a pause in the speaker's train of thought and the
advent of a new perspective. In place of Christ standing in the
Mandorla, we have "das Nichts" standing in the "Mandel," a
word suggested by Mandorla, but having entirely different
associations: Osip Mandelshtam and the Jewish people. The association of the Jews with nothingness, familiar from "Psalm,"
is introduced into the poem. The dash indicates that the speaker,
the first viewer of the picture, is already aware of the complicated implications which he will develop and express in the
course of the poem. His reaction is detached, subdued, the typical
stance assumed by Celan in his poetry. What is in the almond-
halo? Nothing. On the literal level, there is nothing there. On a
symbolic level, the nothingness is reminiscent of God and his
chosen people.[26] The repetition in the final line emphasizes the
constancy of the relationship between the Jews and nothingness.

The structure of the second stanza is parallel to that of the first.
The nature or identity of the king, however, is problematical.
On a metaphysical level, it may suggest God and the Jewish
kings. In any event, on the literal level it alludes to Christ the
King who once stood there in the picture but is now absent. His
presence, however, as we know from so many passages in Celan's
poetry, is still felt by the Jews—as it is still felt in the picture.
The eighth line is generally interpreted as an affirmation of the

"eternity of the Jewish people." Werner Weber, the first inter-
preter of the poem, formulated this view as follows: "Hair which
does not turn gray is removed from the process of aging, placed
above time."[27] The context, however, would seem to demand an
entirely different interpretation. Indentation sets the line apart,
indicating that a further shift in perspective has taken place. In
the Bible, the almond is used to symbolize a gray-haired old
man; the association of almond and gray hair, accordingly, follows quite naturally, given the function of word plays and
associations in the poem. Hair is often associated with death in
Celan, as in "Espenbaum" (MG, 15): "Meiner Mutter Haar
ward nimmer weiß"—because, of course, she was killed in a
concentration camp. The line "Judenlocke, wirst nicht grau"
must have a similar meaning in the present poem.[28] An additional meaning of the line can be seen when the thought of the
preceding stanza is followed: Jewish hair also refers to Christ,
a Jew who died at an early age and whose hair, accordingly, did
not turn gray. This motif, too, is essential to the theme of the
poem.

The chain of associations and word plays continues to grow
more complex in the next stanza. The Hebrew words for "eye"
and "nothing," while spelled differently, are both pronounced
"ayin," as is the Hebrew word for "where." The proximity of
"whither," "eye," and "nothing" suggests the Hebrew language,
and, accordingly, the Jewish people. The first word of the stanza
is "Und"; this unusual beginning indicates that another shift has
taken place. "Wohin steht dein Auge?/ Dein Auge steht der
Mandel entgegen./ ... Es steht zum König." A different kind
of word play is at work here. A hasty reading of these lines will
leave the simple impression that the eye is directed toward the
almond, the nothingness, and the king, which are more or less
identical. But the idioms "entgegenstehen" and "Er steht zu
jemandem" are used very precisely, following the repeated use of
"stehen" in its normal sense. The former means "to be opposed to,"
and the latter "to support." The thou of this stanza is opposed
to the almond and the nothingness, two words used to suggest
the Jews, and supports the king, Christ. The thou stands in contrast to the thou of "Judenlocke, wirst nicht grau" and would
accordingly seem to be the eye of a Gentile. In the present
context of Christ and Christian art, of opposition to the Jews

and support of Christ, it is the eye of a Christian. This Christian thou must be thought of as a second person, perhaps a Christian viewing the picture simultaneously, certainly the Christian reader of the poem.

An additional justification for assuming the juxtaposition Jewish eye—Christian eye can be found in still another meaning of "Mandel." It is used by Celan in compounds such as "Mandelauge" to suggest a Jewish eye. The first two lines of the stanza would then carry the implication that Jew and Christian confront each other here with the Christian opposing the Jew, who is nothing, and supporting the king, who is also nothing, but who has been the ultimate cause of the persecution of the Jews. One is reminded of Elie Wiesel's bitter allusion to Christmas upon hearing the rumor that his camp was to be liberated: "It was not the first time a false prophet had foretold to us peace-on-earth."[29] The Christian looks at the physical void and supports a moral vacuum. The complexity of the word associations is considerable, as is the significance of their implications. In this poem the word "Mandel" is applied to the Jewish people, to the hair of Jews killed in concentration camps, to a Jewish eye (which is contrasted with a Christian eye viewing the picture), then to the Christian halo and, by way of the picture of Christ within it (or which was formerly within it), to Christ himself, ironically a Jew in whose name the Jews have been persecuted.

An examination of the final stanza and some related passages will conclusively establish the negative tone of the poem as well as the validity of the word associations posited in the present intepretation. The single line "Judenlocke, wirst nicht grau" is indented, but initially it seems to be a line of free verse like the remainder of the poem; it could be read with several different stress patterns. But the final two lines comprise a rhymed couplet with identical meter; and this regular meter must also be applied to the earlier line, setting it even further apart. Rhymed couplets are extremely rare except in Celan's earliest poetry, and when they do occur, they usually have a bitter tone. The couplets from "Assisi" (SS, 32),

> Glanz, der nicht trösten will, Glanz.
> Die Toten—sie betteln noch, Franz.

and, most significantly, "Nähe der Gräber," two poems discussed
above, illustrate the role of rhyme in Celan's poetry:

> Und duldest du, Mutter, wie einst, ach, daheim,
> den leisen, den deutschen, den schmerzlichen Reim?

The "Judenlocke" of the earlier line becomes "Menschen-
locke," again establishing a contrast between Jew and Gentile.
As has been observed, the Jews were not considered to be human
by the Nazis, and accordingly the contrast "Jude—Mensch" is
made here. But why should the human hair not turn gray? On
one level, this must surely refer to the previous line and carry
the meaning that Jews are also human beings. A second meaning is related to Christ as God and man. From the Jewish point
of view, Jesus is not God; he is a man who died at an early age,
whose hair did not become gray, and who is now, a man long
dead, quite literally "nothing"—like the rest of the Jews.

There is a further Biblical allusion present. One passage in
which the almond is associated with an old man is Ecclesiastes
12:5, "Also when they shall be afraid of that which is high . . .
and the almond tree shall flourish . . . because man goeth to his
long home, and the mourners go about the streets," and this
allusion leads to a final word association in the poem. Ecclesiastes
12 concludes: "Fear God, and keep his commandments: for this
is the whole duty of man [a literal translation of the German
is: 'for that is the duty of all men']. For God shall bring every
work into judgment, with every secret thing, whether it be good,
or whether it be evil." In other words, given the situation "Jewish
hair, you don't turn gray," because of the concentration camps,
then the "human hair" should also not turn gray—in retribution.
But in the first place, there has been no retribution for the
wrongs done to the Jewish people. And in the second place,
there is the question, whether there should be retribution on
an appropriate scale. The bitterness and frustration of the
dilemma, a major problem in the writings of many contemporary Jewish thinkers, are expressed in the final line.[30]

At the end of the poem the empty almond is again the empty
halo and is described as "königsblau," the color used in art to
portray majesty. The final word, then, returns to the original
reference to art contained in the title. Blue undoubtedly has

PAUL CELAN

TWAYNE PUBLISHERS, INC.
31 UNION SQUARE WEST   NEW YORK, N. Y. 10003

some overtones of the Aryan blue eye as in "Todesfuge." The reference to the Jews is still contained in the word "Mandel." The juxtaposition of "Leere" and "Mandel" suggests, in addition to the meanings discussed above, an allusion to the Jewish concept of the Jewish eye as empty—because it has literally cried itself out as a result of its sufferings. The open syntax of the final line is indicative of the open meaning and the inevitable complexity of associations. It is charged with emotion, but difficult or impossible to describe discursively.

CHAPTER 7

Atemwende

I *General Characteristics*

C ELAN'S next major collection is entitled *Atemwende* (1967). The word occurs only in the title; it is found in none of the poems, unlike the other titles, *Die Niemandsrose, Sprachgitter,* etc., all of which do occur in individual poems. We accordingly lack, in this instance, the context of a poem to suggest possible meanings of the title. One possible implication is clear. "Atem" retains connotations of the Jewish "breath," and "Wende" indicates a turning, perhaps even a turning point. And, indeed, there is a decided change of direction in *Atemwende* vis-à-vis *Die Niemandsrose.* The Jewish element, while still present, is muted almost to the point of silence.

The word "Atemwende" does occur in one of Celan's prose works, the Meridian speech, and the contexts in which it is used there are revealing. After interpreting Lucile's exclamation "Es lebe der König," Celan goes on to discuss the similar attitude which he sees in Büchner's *Lenz*: "Lenz—das heißt Büchner—ist hier einen Schritt weiter gegangen als Lucile. Sein 'Es lebe der König' ist kein Wort mehr, es ist ein furchtbares Verstummen, es verschlägt ihm—und auch uns—den Atem und das Wort. Dichtung: das kann eine Atemwende bedeuten." ("Lenz—that is Büchner, has here gone one step further than Lucile. His 'Long live the king' is no longer a word, it is a terrible falling silent, it takes away his breath and word, and ours too. Poetry: it can represent a resumption and reorientation of breathing," Mer, 81). Later in the same speech Celan returns to the subject: "Zweimal, bei Luciles 'Es lebe der König' und als sich unter Lenz der Himmel als Abgrund auftat, schien die Atemwende da zu sein.... Die Dichtung, meine Damen und Herren,—:diese Unendlich-sprechung von lauter Sterblichkeit und Umsonst!" ("Twice, in

Lucile's 'Long live the king!' and when heaven opened under
Lenz as an abyss, the resumption and reorientation of breathing
seemed to have occurred.... Poetry, ladies and gentlemen, this
declaring of pure mortality and futility to be eternal," Mer, 85).
The "Atemwende" is associated with the rebellion of man against
the absurdity of existence; it is poetry, i.e., the attribution of
eternity to "pure mortality and futility." Since the word implies
defiance, "Wende" would seem to carry connotations of "against,"
as in the term "Gegenwort," from the Meridian speech. It would
imply a continuation of the trend away from, and against, the
past, begun in *Die Niemandsrose*, but a new turn or shift in direction is also suggested.

The book contains six sections or cycles, none of which is
individually titled. But the first of these cycles was published in
1965 in a limited edition, along with eight etchings by Celan's
wife under the title *Atemkristall*. Already in these poems, published less than two years after *Die Niemandsrose*, a definite
change can be noted. The images are almost without exception
difficult and perplexing. A partial explanation of their difficulty
can be found in two additional characteristics of the book: in
place of the longer poems containing several related images and
perhaps a title, which serve to elucidate each other, most of the
poems now are quite short, and very few have titles. There is an
increase in the number of direct references to writing—for
example, the repeated use of "Buchstabe" ("letter of the alpha-
bet," or Hebrew "consonant")—an aspect of the book which has
been strongly emphasized by several critics. But certain other
images also figure prominently, and the references to writing
and speech must be considered in terms of the pattern of imagery
which is developed throughout the collection.

The poems surely do not approach the level of abstract
experiments with language, as some critics have maintained.
Much additional research will have to be done by scholars before
it will be possible to trace and describe all of the themes of the
book. But even now several patterns can be observed. The word
"Wahn" ("delusion," with connotations of "Wahnsinn," "insan-
ity,") occurs more frequently than before, suggesting the author's
own periodic loss of contact with reality. And as Christoph
Perels has observed, "From 'Todesfuge' on, the events of contemporary history can be seen in all of the poet's collections, and

they are not absent in this one."[1] The validity of Perels's assertion
can be demonstrated by listing some passages which clearly call
to mind the ever-present motif of the Jews whose grave is "in
the air": "Mit erdwärts gesungenen Masten/ fahren die Him-
melswracks." ("With earthward-sung masts the heaven-wrecks
travel," AW, 16); "Stehen, im Schatten/ des Wundenmals in der
Luft.// Für-niemand-und-nichts-Stehn." ("Stand in the shadow
of the wound-mark in the sky. Stand-for-no-one-and-nothing,"
AW, 19); "... Rauchspur/ du, droben,/ in Frauengestalt,"
("Smoketrace you up there, in woman's form," AW, 40); "Land-
schaft mit Urnenwesen./ Gespräche/ von Rauchmund zu Rauchmund" ("Landscape with urn-beings. Conversations from smoke-
mouth to smoke-mouth," AW, 55); "(... damals,/ höher als
oben,/ ... grub ich mich in dich und in dich.)" ("then, higher
than up, I dug myself into you and into you," AW, 68).

The reference in the last quotation is perhaps the least obvious
of the allusions to the motif from "Todesfuge," but the associations which are present—the past, the reference to height, and
the final phrase combining "dug" with the repetition of "into you
and into you"—scarcely leave room for doubt. And if there were
still doubt, the context of the poem would dispel it immediately.
The above lines come from the difficult poem "Aschenglorie"
("Ash-glory"). In the first stanza of this poem, the "Aschenglorie"
is said to be "... hinter/ deinen... / Händen am Dreiweg"
("behind your hands at the three-[forked-] road"), and the image
is rephrased in the fourth stanza: "Aschen-/ glorie hinter/
euch Dreiweg-/ Händen" ("Ash-glory behind you three-road-
hands"). Klaus Weissenberger has suggested two meanings for
the image "your hands at the three-forked road," interpreting
the thou as the Jews in the camps and as the poet himself;
(1) for the Jews there was no return (no escape), and the future
held death or the betrayal of fellow Jews; (2) the *ich* cannot
deny the sorrow and pain—he must write about it and he is
at the same time aware that he thereby becomes guilty of
betrayal by virtue of the alienating effect of poetry.[2]

The element of betrayal is, indeed, linked with highly personal
vocabulary in the second stanza: "Pontisches Einstmals: hier,/
ein Tropfen,/ auf/ dem ertrunkenen Ruderblatt,/ tief/ im
versteinerten Schwur,/ rauscht es auf." ("Pontic Once, here,
a drop, on the drowned oar blade, deep in the oath turned to

stone, it rushes up"). The word "pontisch" refers to the Black Sea and in one meaning specifically suggests the area to the north of the sea, the Ukraine, a region familiar from Celan's early poetry. The final lines suggest the breaking of a vow, the incurring of guilt. The use of this motif in "Edgar Jené und der Traum vom Traume" is called to mind: "... Am Hochaltar endlich stand ein Hahn und krähte" ("at the high altar finally a cock stood and crowed"). The reference to the cock which crowed after Peter's denial of Christ clearly establishes the presence of guilt and betrayal in the early essay.

The tone of the final stanza of "Aschenglorie" is very negative and bitter: "Niemand/ zeugt für den/ Zeugen." ("No one bears witness for the witness"). Once again, the beginning of the gospel of St. John is called to mind: "John bare witness of him. ... And this is the record [Zeugnis] of John" (1:15 and 19). "Zeugen"— another word used more frequently in Atemwende than in the poet's previous books—means "to beget" as well as "to bear witness"; sexual connotations are, accordingly, present in this Biblical word, as is often the case. "Niemand" again suggests the absence of God; the speaker is a witness, but no one bears witness for him. The salvation promised by the gospel is implicitly denied by Celan.

Probably the most negative poem of the entire collection is "Osterqualm" ("Easter Smoke," AW, 81). The opening stanza establishes the religious frame of reference—"Oster" means "Easter" and occasionally is applied to Passover—and also immediately introduces the concept of writing: "Osterqualm, flutend, mit/ der buchstabenähnlichen/ Kielspur inmitten." ("Easter smoke, flowing, with the kiel-track like a letter, in the middle"). The somber mood evoked by the word "Qualm" is reinforced in the second and third stanzas: "(Niemals war Himmel./ Doch Meer ist noch, brandrot,/ Meer.)// Wir hier, wir/, überfahrtsfroh, vor dem Zelt,/ wo du Wüstenbrot bukst/ aus mitgewanderter Sprache." ("Never was heaven. But sea still is, fire-red, sea. We here, we, happy about the journey across, before the tent, where you baked desert-bread, out of speech which traveled along.") The formulation of the first line is particularly stark and the implications are clear.

In the second and third lines the combination of the references to Passover, a red sea, desert-bread, a tent and "wandering speech" suggests Exodus, and it would accordingly seem that the word "überfahrtsfroh" might refer to the crossing of the Red Sea by the Israelites. But possible negative implications are suggested by a parallel passage in "Edgar Jené und der Traum vom Traume" which describes the picture "Das rote Meer geht über Land" ("The Red Sea goes over Land")—or "Das Blutmeer geht über Land" as Celan calls it: "Auf nackten Füßen durchwandert das Gespenst des Krieges die Länder.... Vielgestaltet ist es und was ist es jetzt? Ein schwebendes Blutzelt" ("On naked feet the ghost of war wanders over the earth.... It can take on many forms, and what is it now? A floating blood-tent").

The allusion to the crossing of the Red Sea is seen to function merely as an ironic aside when the implications of stanzas six and seven (the final two of the poem) are considered: "Da: der zerbissene/ Ewigkeitsgroschen, zu uns/ heraufgespien durch die Maschen.// Drei Sandstimmen, drei/ Skorpione:/ das Gastvolk, mit uns/ im Kahn." ("There: the chewed-up eternity-coin, spit up to us through the mesh. Three sand-voices, three scorpions: the guest [or: host] people, with us in the boat.") The "journey across" is now seen to refer to Charon's ferryboat which transports the dead to Hades. "Der zerbissene Ewigkeitsgroschen" suggests the ancient custom of placing a coin under the tongue or between the teeth of the dead person, to be used to pay for his fare to "eternity." The reference to "Sandstimmen" reaffirms the identity of the dead suggested earlier in the poem: they are the Jews." Heaven never existed," accordingly in place of an Ascension ("Himmelfahrt"), to be expected after the Resurrection promised by Easter, we have an "Überfahrt" to Hades. The coins are spit upwards. The bodies could not be supplied with them originally, since the Jews were cremated en masse; in "Aschenglorie" the dead *receive* the coins which are spit out, a reversal of the situation in the myth, which confirms the inadequacy of any possible attempt to repair the damage which has been done to the Jews. Financial reparations are, of course, in vain; but so is Celan's poem, another "Ewigkeitsgroschen," an offering for the dead souls, inadequate and too late.

The opening poem, "Du darfst" (AW, 7), introduces the imagery of ice and snow which is to form a leitmotif throughout the entire collection.

Du darfst mich getrost
mit Schnee bewirten:
sooft ich Schulter an Schulter
mit dem Maulbeerbaum schritt durch den Sommer,
schrie sein jüngstes
Blatt.

(Of course you may serve me snow: as often as I strode through
the summer shoulder to shoulder with the mulberry tree, its young-
est leaf screamed.)

As often in Celan, the verb tenses provide an important clue to
the interpretation. The speaker will now accept a life of snow,
because his attempts to live in the summer were unsuccessful.
"Schreien" ("to cry") is an uncommon word in Celan, and when
it is used, it has connotations of discomfort. In one poem there
is the exclamation: "Schrei nicht vor Schmerz" ("Do not cry in
pain," MG, 13), and Celan's description of the picture "Das rote
Meer geht über Land" is introduced as follows: "Wollten wir
nicht den Schrei des Menschen, unseren eigenen Schrei,
vernehmen, lauter als sonst, gellender?" ("Didn't we want to
perceive the cry of man, our own cry, louder than usual, more
piercing?"). Summer on the other hand, is a word of unusually
positive connotations. It suggests a time of hope and promise:
"Sie tragen die Schuld ab ... an ein Wort,/ das zu Unrecht
besteht, wie der Sommer" ("They pay their debt with a word
which exists unjustly like the summer," SS, 49), or: "... wir
fanden/ das Wort, das den Sommer heraufkam:/ Blume." ("We
found the word which came up the summer: flower," SG, 25).
The poem "Du darfst" implies that the hope of summer must
remain unfulfilled: whenever the speaker attempted to live
normally during the summer, nature herself violently objected,
as though his presence were a source of pain. Snow has a negative connotation in Celan. Whereas summer suggests warmth,
growth, companionship, and hope, snow and ice suggest the
opposite. Sometimes snow carries the primary connotation of
silence, as in "Schnee des Verschwiegenen" ("snow of that
which was kept silent") from "Mit wechselndem Schlüssel" (SS,
36). It may also have a more basic meaning, as in the Jené essay:
"Das Nordlicht aber hat jetzt einen Sohn, und Edgar Jené war
der erste, der ihn sah. Da wo der Mensch in den Schneewäldern

seiner Verzweiflung in Fesseln erstarrt ist, kommt er groß vorüber"
("The Northern Lights now have a son and Edgar Jené was the
first to see him. There, where man is frozen in the snow-woods
of his desperation, he passes by, awe-inspiring"). The atmosphere
of loneliness and desolation felt in the painting "Der Sohn des
Nordlichts" and described here by Celan is also present in the
poem "Du darfst."

Many references to snow, ice, and Northern landscapes are
present in *Atemwende,* and many appear as a part of difficult
images: the phrase "In den Flüssen nördlich der Zukunft" ("In
the rivers to the north of the future," AW, 10), for example,
explicitly combines space (north), time (future), and a concrete object (rivers). The phrase "Nordwahr. Südhell" ("North-
true. South-bright," AW, 24) suggests a contrast similar to that
between summer and snow, and implies that the one is true and
bleak, whereas the other is bright and false. A similar mood is
established by the lines "der/ Herr dieser Stunde/ war/ ein
Wintergeschöpf, ihm/ zulieb/ geschah, was geschah—" ("The
Lord of this hour was a winter-creature; what happened happened for his sake," (AW, 40).

II   *Three Poems*

The examples of winter imagery given above will serve as an
introduction to the last poems of the first cycle. As H. G. Gadamer
has pointed out, the final three poems form a loose-knit unit.[3]
The first and the third are longer than average but are otherwise
quite typical in their images and style. The short middle poem,
on the other hand, is quite atypical. It is "(Ich kenne dich"
(AW, 26).

> (Ich kenne dich, du bist die tief Gebeugte,
> ich, der Durchbohrte, bin dir untertan.
> Wo flammt ein Wort, das für uns beide zeugte?
> Du-ganz, ganz wirklich. Ich-ganz Wahn.)

(I know you. You are the one deeply bowed. I, the one pierced
through, am subject to you. Where does there flame a word which
would bear witness for both of us? You, completely, completely real,
I completely delusion.)

The first two lines establish the basic frame of reference by alluding to the "Pietà"; the speaker, then, is Christ, and the thou is Mary, his mother. The first half of the third line contains an allusion to Benn's poem "Ein Wort," "Ein Wort—ein Glanz, ein Flug, ein Feuer,/ Ein Flammenwurf..," and the second half of the line recalls the conclusion of "Aschenglorie," "Niemand/ zeugt für den Zeugen." A second, autobiographical identity of the speaker is thereby established. The final line confirms the transfer of identity from Christ and Mary to Celan and his mother. The mother is "real" to such an extent that her condition determines the nature of the speaker's existence (he is "subject" to her). The thought is similar to that expressed in the early poem "Der Reisekamerad" ("The Travel Companion," MG, 64), where the poetic word is called the "Mündel" ("ward") of the mother. The speaker's existence, as a result of the mother's fate, is characterized by the word "Wahn." The use of rhyme in the poem further emphasizes the intimate theme and supports the conclusion that the poet can find no "word," no poem which can satisfy, can do justice to, both himself and the Jewish victims, or, in this case specifically the dead mother.

The first of the three poems, "Wortaufschüttung" ("Word-out-spewing," AW, 25), combines direct references to language with faint suggestions of religious themes. Klaus Weissenberger establishes a reference to the Christian cross in the image "der flutende Mob/ ... Abbild und Nachbild/ kreuzen eitel zeithin." ("the flowing mob... reproduction and copy cross vainly time-wards"), and observes that the "mob is satisfied with the imitation of the cross and disposes of its message in a careless manner." Weissenberger offers the following explanation of the final image of the poem, "die Königs-/ geburten": "Celan alludes to the patriarchal age of Judaism in which the connection between God and the Kings was maintained and, accordingly, Kings were born. The present time is ruled by the mob and births of Kings remain— as indicated by the hyphen—almost hypothetical."[4] The final lines of "Tübingen, Jänner" ("Tübingen, January," NR, 24), could be cited in support of the interpretation; if a Patriarch were to come into the world today he would be helpless. Celan seems to make no fundamental distinction between Kings and Patriarchs in these poems. The implications of the references to Judaism and Christianity in "Wortaufschüttung" and "(Ich kenne

dich" are certainly not as unambiguous as are the references
in such poems as "Tenebrae" and "Mandorla." But the general
tone is clear; the promises of hope offered by both Judaism and
Christianity have not materialized. The mob's "idle crossing"
refers to the lasting heritage of the birth of Christ, the last of the
Kings. The speaker, seeing himself as a Christ-figure, is unable
to find a "flaming word" compatible with both himself and his
dead mother. The "Ewigkeitsgroschen" which he attempts to
spit up to her is unsatisfactory.

The tentative answer to the complex problem is given in
"Weggebeizt" (AW, 27).[5]

> Weggebeizt vom
> Strahlenwind deiner Sprache
> das bunte Gerede des An-
> erlebten--das hundert-
> züngige Mein-
> gedicht, das Genicht.
>
> Aus-
> gewirbelt,
> frei
> der Weg durch den menschen-
> gestaltigen Schnee,
> den Büßerschnee, zu
> den gastlichen
> Gletscherstuben und -tischen.
>
> Tief
> in der Zeitenschrunde,
> beim
> Wabeneis
> wartet, ein Atemkristall,
> dein unumstößliches
> Zeugnis.

(Eroded by the ray-wind of your language, the garish chatter of
that which was inauthentically experienced—the hundred-tongued
my-poem, the lie-noem.//Swirled out, the road free through the
human-formed snow, the penitent-snow, to the hospitable glacier
rooms and tables.//Deep in the time-crevice, by the honeycomb-ice
waits a breath-crystal, your irrefutable testimony.)

The highly problematical first stanza takes up the question posed
in "(Ich kenne dich,": where does a word flame which bears

witness for both mother and son? The reference to the "garish chatter of that which was inauthentically experienced" seems to allude to Celan's own early attempts to come to terms with the past in elaborate, colorful metaphors. The prefix "Mein-" suggests primarily possession, "my"; it is also an old root signifying "false," and is still present in the modern word "Meineid" (perjury, false oath). The obvious connection between "Mein-Gedicht" and "Meineid" suggests the broken oath mentioned in "Edgar Jené und der Traum vom Traume," and is also reminiscent of two lines from "Aschenglorie": "Tief/ im versteinerten Schwur" ("Deep in the stone-hardened oath"). A similarity in sound leads now from one neologism to another, from "Mein-gedicht" to "Genicht"; the substitution of "n" for "d" in the word "Gedicht" produces a word which would roughly mean "nothing"; "poem—noem" is the English equivalent found by most translators.

The second stanza is much more easily accessible. It refers back directly to the first poem of the cycle, "Du darfst mich getrost mit Schnee bewirten." The image of a guest being entertained is common to both poems, and the landscape of each is reminiscent of that depicted in the Jené essay when Celan describes "Der Sohn des Nordlichts": "der Mensch in den Schneewäldern seiner Verzweiflung." The possibility of a community, of social intercourse, is denied. The only host which the speaker will have is winter; he will sit alone at the tables of ice. The third stanza introduces another of the many images combining time ("Zeit"), space ("tief"), and objects ("Schrunde"). The "goal" is the "Atemkristall," a combination which suggests the Jewish "spirit" as well as loneliness and sterility. An allusion to Adalbert Stifter's story *Bergkristall* (*Mountain-crystal*) is probably implied. In Stifter's story, two children become lost and take refuge in an icy cave one stormy Christmas Eve. They are rescued, and the story affirms the redeeming power of Christmas. The third stanza also establishes a connection with the previous poem. The final word, "Zeugnis," answers the question, "What will bear witness for us both?" No *word* which flames, but a cold, lifeless *breath*-crystal. The Jewish "Atem" is affirmed over the Christian word, but the solace which is offered is not great. In fact, the power of the poem, which is considerable, is largely dependent on the tension between the bleakness of the answer and the certainty with which the answer is given.

III   "Keine Sandkunst mehr"

Another poem which combines references to Judaism and the poet's relationship to it with an enigmatic word play is "Keine Sandkunst mehr" (AW, 35).

> Keine Sandkunst mehr, kein Sandbuch, keine Meister.
>
> Nichts erwürfelt. Wieviel
> Stumme?
> Siebenzehn.
>
> Deine Frage--deine Antwort.
> Dein Gesang, was weiß er?
>
> Tiefimschnee,
>   ·   Iefimnee,
>   I-i-e.

(No more sand-art, no sand-book, no masters.//The dice yield nothing. How many silent ones? Seventeen.//Your question--your answer. Your song, what does it know?// Deep-in-snow, eep-in-ow, e-i-o.)

Peter Mayer associates the first line with the sand of *Der Sand aus den Urnen,* as does Jürgen P. Wallmann, who further suggests that the "Meister" refers to the phrase "der Tod ist ein Meister aus Deutschland" from "Todesfuge."[6] The second stanza refers to the Eighteen-Prayer, allusion to which is also made in Celan's first cycle from his first book, "An den Toren." One of the seventeen poems in the cycle contains the following line: "Leer blieb der letzte, der achtzehnte Krug" (SU, 20). The Eighteen-Prayer, expressing hope of salvation and trust in God, was broken off in the earlier poem after the first seventeen parts; the poet could not express the affirmation which completion of the prayer would have implied. Now even these seventeen are silent, suggesting a total dissatisfaction, on the part of the speaker, with his past relationship to the Jewish tradition. The third stanza refers to the problem posed in the question, "Wo flammt ein Wort, das für uns beide zeugte?" and the answer contained in "Weggebeizt," the "Atemkristall." The song, the poet's previous poems, have offered no solution. The answer,

again reminiscent of "Weggebeizt," is given in the word "Tiefim-
schnee," a restatement of the basic mood of earlier images, such
as "mit Schnee bewirten."

As critics point out, the reduction of the word to "I-i-e" suggests a movement away from communication and toward silence.
This is certainly one function of the unusual poetic device of
removing the consonants and leaving only the basic vowels of the
three words, long "i," short "i," and long "e." The speaker is
encased in his showy landscape and moves away from the communication typical of a more conventional society. A further
reference to Judaism in the final words brings together the three
themes of the poem: the turning away from the earlier mode of
dealing with Judaism, the snow imagery, and the loss of com-
municative power. The removal of consonants from a word is a
reversal of the standard Hebrew practice of omitting the vowels
in written texts. Celan is, accordingly, alluding to this trait of
the language, and to his own earlier use of it in incorporating
Hebrew word plays in his poetry, one last example of "Sandkunst" which is now being rejected and which the poet will
utilize no more.

IV   "Einmal"

The final poem of the book is "Einmal" (AW, 103):

> Einmal,
> da hörte ich ihn,
> da wusch er die Welt,
> ungesehn, nachtlang,
> wirklich.
>
> Eins und Unendlich,
> vernichtet,
> ichten.
>
> Licht war. Rettung.

(Once, I heard him there, he washed the world there, unseen, all
night long, really.//One and infinite, destroyed, *ichten*.//Light was.
Salvation.)

The religious frame of reference has been perceptively noted by Wilhelm Höck: "Washing has the meaning of baptizing (which, according to Paul, follows upon the death of Jesus Christ)."[7] Höck goes on to offer his interpretation, with which I do not agree: "Light and Salvation proceed from this baptism-in-death." As I see it, the saving power of washing seems rather to be negated in the poem. The word "wirklich" is rare in Celan's poetry and its use in "(Ich kenne dich" comes to mind, where the greatest, indeed the only, "reality" is death. A similar negative tone is implied in "Einmal." The effects of Christ's death and Christian baptism have, for the Jews, been "real," that is, dangerous and even deadly. The meaning of the unusual word "ichten" in the second stanza is problematical. Several possibilities exist: (1) it may refer to the Middle High German word "iht," the opposite of "nicht," and would then mean "to exist, to have substance" (probably third person plural, present tense); (2) it may be formed from the verb "ichen," "to I," and would in this case be the past tense; (3) it may suggest a loose connection between the words immediately above and below it, "vernichtet" and "Licht." I feel that it is impossible to limit the meaning of the word here; all meanings inherent in the word "ichten" are active in the present context.

The difference between the three stanzas of the poem is striking. The first one seems typical of one of Celan's techniques; it contains a pronoun without a definite antecedent, as well as images which seem to carry religious connotations. The second stanza is also typical of one of the poet's techniques. The language is extremely condensed, and the thought is equally complicated. "One and endless," both "destroyed," are the subject of "ichten," a verb with a wealth of meanings and impossible to translate. The final one-line stanza, on the other hand, seems to be quite simple. This discrepancy alone is an indication that the statement is not to be taken at face value. Celan's solution at this stage of his career is in no way simple, nor can it be stated in simple terms. Even though "Rettung" is not the theological term for "salvation," the line is surely ironic. Allusion is made to the beginning of the gospel of St. John, where Christ, the Light, shines in the darkness and John the Baptist, the harbinger of Christ, baptizes with water, foreshadowing salvation. There was indeed light; but for the Jews, at least, there was no solace. The contrast between the linguistic complexities of the second stanza and the simplicity of the third suggests a similar contrast between the complexity—the absurdity—of history and the simplicity of the traditional Christian solution. This ironic line is Celan's "Atemwende," his "Es lebe der König," his attempt to affirm the absurdity of life by means of a completely absurd statement which, like Lucile's exclamation, can be—and in fact is—taken literally as an affirmation of a bygone era.

CHAPTER 8

The Late Poems

I General Characteristics

IN the fifteen years between 1948 and 1963, Celan published a total of five volumes of poetry, the books appearing regularly at intervals of three or four years. The average number of poems contained in each collection is less than fifty. In 1967 *Atemwende* was published. The pattern of one book every four years remained intact, but in one respect the previous pattern was broken: *Atemwende* contained a total of seventy-eight poems, far more than were to be found in any of the previous collections. Celan's productivity continued to increase; new collections followed in 1968 (*Fadensonnen, Thread-suns*), 1970 (*Lichtzwang, Light-compulsion*), and 1971 (*Schneepart, Snow-part*). The average number of poems contained in the last three books is more than eighty. In addition, Celan published four books of verse translations in 1967 and 1968, and two limited editions, *Todtnauberg* and *Schwarzmaut*, containing poems which were to be included in *Lichtzwang*, were issued in 1968 and 1969, respectively. The late poems, to be sure, tend to be shorter than even those of *Die Niemandsrose* (1963). But, nonetheless, a significant increase in productivity on Celan's part can definitely be seen during the last three or four years of his life.

It is often difficult to make distinctions between the last three books of poetry. Although Celan died approximately two months prior to the appearance of *Lichtzwang*, he made the arrangements for the book's publication. *Schneepart*, on the other hand, is truly a "posthumous" collection. According to the publisher, the manuscript of the book was found completely assembled among the poet's papers following his death, but he himself never sent it in for publication. The poems were written in 1967 and 1968, i.e., before those contained in *Lichtzwang* and presumably at the same time as, or very shortly after, those in

Fadensonnen. Thus it is impossible to discuss the last three collections in terms of a chronological progression.

The tendency toward condensation noted in *Atemwende* is accentuated in the poems of the final three books. The poems are almost without exception difficult and many of them seem to defy explication. But here, as in *Atemwende,* it would be improper to describe the poems as linguistic games or semantic experiments. A definite emotional force is consistently present, if often difficult to describe precisely. The vagueness of the language frequently seems to be a corroboration of the emotional content: the reader repeatedly senses a lack of direction in the poems. Two stylistic traits which are very important in the late poems will illustrate this facet. The first is the frequency of the references to numbers, and especially to fractions, in unusual contexts; fragmentation is often suggested. Some examples of this are: "Ein Halbschmerz, ein zweiter, ohne/ Dauerspur, halbwegs/ hier. Eine Halblust." ("A half-pain, a second, without permanent traces, halfway here. A half-joy," FS, 95), and "die halb-/ beschrittenen Knüppel-/ pfade im Hochmoor," ("the half-trod wooden paths in the high-moor," LZ, 30). The second device, which was also observed in *Atemwende,* is the strange use of spatial adverbs, especially prefixes of separable verbs, to suggest, paradoxically, a lack of direction, at least in relation to the physical world: "alles/ ging um,/ entsiegelt wie wir" ("everything went around, unsealed like ourselves," FS, 110), and "die Brauen,/ ... schon fortgeschwungen aus der Flocke Welt,/ nicht hin, nicht her." ("The brows already thrust away, out of the world a flake, not in this direction nor in that one," LZ, 87.) Although the relationship between the poems and the actual physical world becomes more tenuous, the late poems contain a large number of direct references to specific places: Paris (FS, 76; LZ, 72; SP, 51; etc.); Frankfurt, FS 8; and Lyon, FS, 24 are but a few of the many examples which could be listed. Two poems in *Schneepart* are entitled "Für Eric," "For Eric," the poet's son. Such direct personal involvement in a poem has not been seen since the very early poems which are addressed to the poet's dead mother.

The apparently unrelated traits of the later poems which were just mentioned do in fact, when taken together, suggest a trend: they indicate a desperate search for direction. The lack of any consistent direction in the poems becomes apparent when the variety of approaches used in them is considered. Whereas previously Celan tended to produce a smaller number of poems which he assembled in cycles and collections having at least a degree of consistency and unity, now short fragmentary poems, having greatly divergent themes and emotional content, are thrown out in large numbers.

Many references to the Judaic past are still present in the final three collections. One reviewer has even associated the image "Fadensonnen" with the first chapters of Genesis.[1] Numerous individual words which relate to Jewish themes could be cited: "Sabbatkerzen" ("Sabbath Candles," SP, 64) and "der/ sechzehnte Psalm ("the sixteenth Psalm," SP, 66) are but two examples. Hans Mayer interprets two poems in terms of a concentration camp experience, and many others could be analyzed in this manner.[2] An especially interesting and complicated use of Jewish sources is seen in the poem "Du sei wie du" ("You be like you," LZ, 101).[3] The poem quotes the medieval German mystic Meister Eckhart in the original Middle High German: "Stand up Jerusalem and raise yourself . . . and be illuminated." The poem then closes with a stanza, consisting of two Hebrew words "kumi/ ori," which alludes to the original source of the Middle High German quotation. Meister Eckhart's words come originally from Isaiah 51:17, and Celan's Hebrew phrase is taken from Isaiah 60:1 and means "Arise, shine." Eckhart, as he himself says in the context from which the quotations were taken, read the Old Testament in Latin, the language of the Christian Church. Celan uses the original Hebrew to suggest his own allegiance to the original Jewish tradition, thereby implicitly denying the Christian interpretation of Isaiah as a prophecy of the coming of Christ.

The closing lines from two poems will demonstrate the continuing presence, in these late poems, of images and themes developed in the earlier works, and will also illustrate the different moods which can be found in the late poetry. "Auch mich" ("Also me," LZ, 85), begins with a negative statement in the first stanza: ". . . Keine Hand,/ . . . wirft mir ein Glück in die Stunde . . ." ("No hand makes my hour more pleasant"). The second and third stanzas each begin with the word "doch," indicating a contradiction of something expressed or implied in the preceding statement: "Doch stehen die Zahlen bereit, der Träne zu leuchten" ("But the numbers stand ready to shine for the tear"). The final stanza is: "Und die Mandelhode/ gewittert/ und blüht." ("And the almond-testicle thunders and blooms.") As so often, a sexual reference is used in conjunction with a word referring to the Jews, suggesting in the present poem the blossoming following the storm, the increasing strength and vitality of the Jewish people.

An entirely different kind of poem is "Lila Luft" ("Lilac Air," SP, 9). The images of the first part of the poem are quite obscure, in contrast to the final stanza which is clear and unambiguous in its repetition and confirmation of the mood of "Du darfst mich getrost/ mit Schnee bewirten:" the lines are: "von der/ Stehkneipe zur/ Schneekneipe" ("from the stand-up tavern to the snow tavern"). The speaker feels isolated and alone; he withdraws from the intimate convivial atmosphere of the tavern to the solitude of the "glacier tables" of his snow tavern, which was also previously mentioned in the poem "Weggebeizt" (AW, 27).

Poems of optimism and affirmation are not uncommon, especially in *Fadensonnen*, and this spirit can undoubtedly be explained, in many instances, on the basis of Celan's reaction to the Six Days' War of June, 1967. Celan was, to be sure, no Zionist. But Jews from all over the world, regardless of the firmness of their religious convictions or their previous commitment to Israel, rallied behind the Israelis upon the outbreak of the war. Elie Wiesel, for example, immediately flew to Jerusalem from New York when he heard that the war had begun, and he later used his experiences as the basis for the novel *Beggar in Jerusalem*. The fear of still another Jewish defeat, one which would have destroyed the young state of Israel, was intensely felt during the war by Jews everywhere. And a correspondingly great feeling of exhilaration was experienced following the military victory over the Arab states, which restored the Holy City Jerusalem to Jewish control for the first time in two thousand years, and which seemed to offer a solid confirmation of the end of many centuries of persecution; the Jewish people, the "Wandering Jew," seemed at last to have found a home.

II *Two Poems*

An analysis of two poems from *Fadensonnen* will illustrate the optimism found in some of the later poems. The first, "Denk dir" ("Just Think," FS, 121), was first published in the *Neue Zürcher Zeitung* of June 24, 1967, and seems clearly to refer to the Jewish victory in the war.

> Denk dir:
> der Moorsoldat von Massada
> bringt sich Heimat bei, aufs
> unauslöschlichste,
> wider
> allen Dorn im Draht.
>
> Denk dir:
> die Augenlosen ohne Gestalt
> führen dich frei durchs Gewühl, du
> erstarkst und
> erstarkst.
>
> Denk dir: deine
> eigene Hand
> hat dies wieder
> ins Leben empor-
> gelittene
> Stück
> bewohnbarer Erde
> gehalten.
>
> Denk dir:
> das kam auf mich zu,
> namenwach, handwach
> für immer,
> vom Unbestattbaren her.

(Just think: the moor-soldier of Massada acquires a home, permanently, counter to all the barbs in the wire.//Just think: the eyeless ones without form lead you free through all the tumult, you grow stronger and stronger.//Just think: your own hand has held this piece of inhabitable earth, which once more suffered up into life.//Just think: that came to me, name-awake, hand-awake, for ever, from where burial is impossible.)

The two references in the first stanza are readily identifiable.[4] "Moorsoldat" is an allusion to one of the best-known songs of the German concentration camps, and Masada is the name of a Jewish outpost in the Palestinian desert, the final fortress to fall to the Romans during the Jewish war in 70 A.D. The first cycle of *Mohn und Gedächtnis* comes immediately to mind. The opening poem of the cycle, "Ein Lied in der Wüste," alludes to the events of the Jewish war, and the final poem, "Corona," in conjunction with "Todesfuge," calls attention to the cyclical nature of Jewish suffering, which culminates in the Nazi death camps. At last the homeless people who lived the life of the "Wandering Jew" from Calvary to Auschwitz has found a home. The chain of events, unbroken from the time of the soldiers of Masada to that of the inmates who sang the song of the "Moorsoldat," has been broken. The final line of the stanza brings together the different ages by means of the various implications of "Dorn"; it suggests both the continuous past sufferings (as is implied in the use of the rose blooming above the thorn in the final stanza of "Psalm," and elsewhere) and, because of the reference to barbed wire, the recent terrors of the concentration camps.

The second stanza begins with another image which combines allusions to the Jewish tradition and the death camps. The "eyeless ones without form" suggest both the victims of the Nazis and the Jews of all ages whose constant weeping has rendered them "eyeless." The dead are now leading the thou to freedom, to a transcendence of the chaos of the past. The thou is here the Jewish people as a whole, who continue to grow stronger and stronger. The third stanza seems to refer directly to the land of Israel, to the actual military victory of the Jewish people which assured the survival of the nation. The birth, or rebirth, of the Jewish nation was difficult to effect, but now it is an established fact. And, most significantly, the Jews did it all by themselves, as the speaker maintains: "your own hands held this piece of earth." A reference to Genesis and to Celan's own poem "Psalm" seems to be present here. God is not able— or willing—to create life anew for the Jews. But they themselves, through suffering and perseverance, have now brought new life to a piece of earth, not to the earthly remains of the dead, who can never be brought back to life, but rather to the soil of a nation.

In the final stanza the speaker says that he has become aware of the implications which have come to him. The phrase "vom Unbestattbaren" refers to the millions of victims who can never have a proper burial. Their sufferings have made the new home-land possible, but they can never be interred in it. Although the frame of reference of the third and fourth lines is vague, the combination of "name," "hand," and "awake" suggests the role of the poet. The wrongs of the past are still present and cannot be rectified. But these wrongs now seem to have acquired at least a degree of meaning and even of value by virtue of the victory in the war, and the poet can find some grounds for affir-mation in them.

The central structural feature of the poem is the repetition of the phrase "denk dir." The words themselves, like the English "just think," imply that the speaker accepts as true something which he would not have thought probable. The tone of the poem is restrained throughout; phrases like "aufs unauslösch-lichste," "erstarkst und/ erstarkst," and others, suggest the depth of feeling conveyed, yet there is no trace of the ecstatic joy which might have been expected. The memory of the dead requires the dignified tone. The victory was made possible only through their sufferings, and the song of celebration is appro-priately thoughtful and restrained. The final word of the poem is the separable prefix "her." Here the prefix fixes the direction; as always, everything in the poet's consciousness comes from the realm of the victims whose grave is in the air. In this case cir-cumstances permit the creation of a rare poem of affirmation.

A second poem of affirmation is "Nah, im Aortenbogen" (FS, 96), which also seems to be based upon the Israeli victory in the Six Days' War:

> Nah, im Aortenbogen,
> im Hellblut:
> das Hellwort.
>
> Mutter Rahel
> weint nicht mehr.
> Rübergetragen
> alles Geweinte.

> Still, in den Kranzarterien,
> unumschnürt:
> Ziw, jenes Licht.

(Near, in the arch of the aorta, in the bright blood: the bright word.//Mother Rachel weeps no more. All that was cried is carried across.//Quiet, in the coronary arteries, unentwined: *Ziw*, that light.)

The combination of allusions and images present in this poem is typical of Celan.[5] The middle stanza refers to a Jewish legend which is based upon the Biblical figure Rachel, especially the references to her in Jeremiah 31:15 and Ruth 4:11. Rachel, the first among the women upon whom the house of Israel is built, is said to have risen from her grave during a dark period of Jewish history and begged God to save her "children," the Jewish people. God was moved and promised her that Israel would be restored. Now, in the poem, Mother Rachel no longer must weep for her children, since they have been delivered. The first and third stanzas are based upon an elaborate heart image, expressed in scientific terminology. The "bright" blood refers to the color of the fresh, life-giving blood of the aorta which has just left the heart. A "bright word" is present here in this blood, near the heart. The final line of the poem contains another reference to Judaism. "Ziw" is the supernatural "light" of the Schechina—roughly, the presence of God—from the writings of the Jewish mystics. In the poem, it is located in the coronary arteries which lead from the aorta to the heart muscles. It is the blood supplied by these arteries which keeps the heart functioning properly. "Unumschnürt," literally "unentwined," alludes to the heart disorder *angina pectoris*, a constriction of the heart. Celan's word is suggested by the etymological root of *angina*, "to strangle." Hence in the present image the heart is freed of the threat of angina, of strangulation, by the blood in the arteries.

The bright word present in the bright, life-giving blood is "Ziw, that light." Another reference to the gospel of John is present here. Point by point the poem denies the development of John's argument. The blood and heart suggest the "life" of the gospel account, and Celan's light is indeed life-giving, as was noted above. But the word of the poem is not the Christian "life" which was the "light of the world, the light of men," the light which "shineth in the darkness." It is in the "bright blood," not in the darkness, and it is now the light of Jewish mysticism, not of the Christian Word.

The association of heart imagery with the "Ziw" is based on a metaphor which is found in the mystical tradition; it is associated with the light of the Schechina, which is the heart of Judaism. But the older mystical, or even Romantic, use of the heart has been replaced by modern scientific terminology. The poet thereby places the life-giving light squarely in the present: it is the continuing vitality of the Jewish traditions. The thought is similar to that of a line from "Corona": "Es ist Zeit.../ daß der Unrast ein Herz schlägt" ("It is time that a heart beat for unrest"). The heart indeed is now beating, and the Jewish people have been freed of their restlessness. But although the older wish and image are still valid, the home is new, and hence new variations of the image are found to express the poet's reaction. It is, of course, impossible to determine to what extent the emotions expressed in this poem, and in "Denk dir," are genuine; they were certainly not lasting, as Celan's suicide some three years later conclusively demonstrates.

CHAPTER 9

A Concluding Note

PAUL Celan was quite familiar with the trends of the literature of Western Europe. He was especially fond of many of the modern French poets. In addition he knew the literature of Eastern Europe, which he was in many cases able to read in the original languages. But he was also a Jewish writer, thoroughly immersed in the Scriptures and in the Jewish literary tradition. Many critics tend to ignore the fact that Jews have their own religious and literary traditions, and that these are reflected in the symbolism and even in the structure of the language used by Jewish poets. Hermann Hakel stresses the importance of this difference in the "Nachwort" to his anthology *Die Bibel im deutschen Gedicht*: "Of course significant differences, in frame of reference and in manner of thinking, can be observed when the poems of Germans are compared with those of German-speaking Jews (and much could be said on this subject)."[1] When Celan used words and images which apparently derive from the Western European literary tradition, allusions to his Jewish heritage are usually also present. Non-Jewish readers tend to recognize only the former aspects of Celan's symbolism.

Once the importance of Celan's Jewishness is established, the nature of his interpretation of Jewish history must be established. As an anonymous reviewer recently observed, Celan "makes us aware of the horror of our age in a way that is the more powerful for being oblique."[2] The essential element of his poems is this grappling with the horrors of our age. His images reflect the atrocities of the distant and recent past and the bleakness of the present. His conclusions are not pleasant. To some extent, these images can be explained, and I have attempted to clarify them and make them more intelligible whenever possible. But they must never be taken too literally

155

or be limited to a certain specific meaning. The effectiveness of Celan's poetry, which is considerable, depends, to a large extent, on his ability to capture a multiplicity of meanings in an image or cluster of images. Only when the reader has become aware of the many possible references and meanings within a poem is he able to "appreciate" the poem—in both senses of the word. Celan's poetry is well worth the effort which is required to gain access to it and read it meaningfully.

Notes and References

Chapter One

1. *Die Wandlung*, 4 (1949), 284.
2. See the reports by Reinhard Döhl, "Geschichte und Kritik eines Angriffs: Zu den Behauptungen gegen Paul Celan," *Jahrbuch der deutschen Akademie für Sprache und Dichtung* 1960 (Heidelberg: Lambert Schneider, 1961), pp. 101-32, and Erhard Schwandt, "Korrekturen zum Bericht von Reinhard Döhl," *Jahrbuch der deutschen Akademie* 1966 (Heidelberg: Lambert Schneider, 1967), pp. 191-99. Celan himself apparently felt much more confident of the support of the Austrian writers than of their German counterparts.
3. *Baubudenpoet*, 1 (1959/60), 115f.
4. The dates of composition of many poems are given in Paul Celan, *Gedichte. Eine Auswahl* (Frankfurt: S. Fischer, 1961).
5. James K. Lyon, "Nature. Its Ideas and Use in the Poetic Imagery of Ingeborg Bachmann, Paul Celan, and Karl Krolow" (diss., Harvard, 1962), p. 86; Peter Mayer, *Paul Celan als jüdischer Dichter* (diss., Heidelberg, 1969), p. 12.
6. Klaus Demus agrees that the explanation given above is accurate, at least as a rough outline.
7. Hans Mayer, "Erinnerung an Paul Celan," *Merkur* 24 (1970), 1158.
8. Elie Wiesel, *Night* (New York: Avon Books, 1969), p. 124.
9. Johannes Firges, *Die Gestaltungsschichten in der Lyrik Paul Celans ausgehend vom Wortmaterial* (diss., Cologne, 1959); see also Firges, "Sprache und Sein in der Dichtung Paul Celans," *Muttersprache*, 72 (1962), 261-69; and James K. Lyon, "The Poetry of Paul Celan. An Approach," *Germanic Review*, 39 (1964), 50-67.
10. Lyon, "Nature," p. 174.
11. Peter Paul Schwarz, *Totengedächtnis und dialogische Polarität in der Lyrik Paul Celans* (Düsseldorf: Schwann, 1966); Siegbert Prawer, "Paul Celan," *Essays on Contemporary German Literature*, ed. B. Keith-Smith (London: O. Wolff, 1966), pp. 161-84.
12. Joachim Schulze, "Mystische Motive in Paul Celans Gedichten," *Poetica*, 3 (1970), 472-509; see also Peter Mayer, "Paul Celan als jüdischer Dichter," *Emuna Horizonte*, 5 (1970), 190-95.
13. Mayer, "Paul Celan," *Emuna Horizonte*, p. 190.
14. Mayer, *Paul Celan*, diss., p. 26.

15. Mayer, "Paul Celan," *Emuna Horizonte,* p. 191.

16. Wiesel, *Night,* p. 92.

17. *Ibid.,* pp. 43f.

18. Elie Wiesel, "Appointment with Hate," *Legends of our Time* (New York: Avon Books, 1970), pp. 177-78.

19. Richard Rubenstein, *After Auschwitz* (Indianapolis: Bobbs-Merrill, 1966), p. 3.

20. Conrad Moehlmann, *The Christian-Jewish Tragedy* (Rochester, N. Y.: Leo Hart, 1933), pp. vii and ix.

21. Götz Wienold, "Paul Celans Hölderlin-Widerruf," *Poetica,* 2 (1968), 216-28.

Chapter Two

1. See *Handwörterbuch des deutschen Aberglaubens* (Berlin and Leipzig: de Gruyter, 1934f.), VI, cols. 1118-20.

2. Jené wrote, in a letter to the author dated December 5, 1971, "Celan felt a certain affinity with the picture, and said that he himself was the Son of the Northern Lights."

3. *Almanach der librairie Flinker* (Paris, 1958); reprinted in *Über Paul Celan,* ed. D. Meinecke (Frankfurt: Suhrkamp, 1970), p. 23; my quotations follow the latter source.

4. 2nd ed. (Munich: List, 1961), pp. 86f.

5. Gottfried Benn, *Gesammelte Werke,* I (Wiesbaden: Limes, 1959), p. 495.

6. *34 x erste Liebe,* ed. Robert Neumann (Frankfurt: Barmeier & Nikel, 1966), pp. 32f.

7. Horst Bienek, "Kein Bekenntnis zum Zeitgedicht," *Neue Rundschau,* 79 (1968), 359.

8. Quotations follow the text in Paul Celan, *Ausgewählte Gedichte,* ed. Beda Allemann (Frankfurt: Suhrkamp, 1968), pp. 127-29.

9. *Gedichte* (Stuttgart: Klett, 1957), pp. 174-76.

10. Rudolph Alexander Schröder, *Gesammelte Werke,* I (Frankfurt: Suhrkamp, 1952), p. 489. A poem entitled "Bremen"—Celan mentioned the name of the city twice in his short address—contains the following lines addressed to the city: "You stand, the sanctuary of freedom,/ and provide a refuge for the honor of the Fatherland" (p. 503).

11. O. Pöggeler, " '. . . Ach, die Kunst,' " *Über Paul Celan,* ed. D. Meinecke (Frankfurt: Suhrkamp, 1970), p. 79.

12. Hans Mayer, "Erinnerung," p. 1154.

13. Peter Mayer noted the significance of this passage; see *Paul Celan,* diss., p. 173.

14. Hans Mayer, "Erinnerung," pp. 1151-52.

15. Quotations follow the text in Paul Celan, *Ausgewählte Gedichte*, ed. Klaus Reichert (Frankfurt: Suhrkamp, 1970), pp. 181-86. A thorough interpretation is given by Renate Böschenstein-Schäfer, "Anmerkungen zu Paul Celans 'Gespräch im Gebirg,'" *Über Paul Celan*, ed. D. Meinecke (Frankfurt: Suhrkamp, 1970), pp. 226-38.

16. Peter Mayer, *Paul Celan*, diss., p. 107; the Biblical quotation is a translation of Cohen's wording.

17. Jakob Soetendorp, *Symbolik der jüdischen Religion* (Gütersloh: Mohn, 1963), p. 136.

Chapter Three

1. Wiesel, *Legends of our Time*, pp. 171f.

2. See Peter Mayer's detailed comments on this section of the poem in *Paul Celan*, diss., pp. 13f.

3. *Altjüdisches Schrifttum ausserhalb der Bibel*, tr. and with a commentary by Paul Riessler, 2nd ed. (Heidelberg: Kerle, 1966), p. 10. The prayer exists in more than one form, not all of which have eighteen parts. Celan seems to be alluding to the title and the text in the form quoted here.

4. Martin Buber, *Werke*, III (Munich: Kösel, 1963), p. 528.

5. Prawer, "Paul Celan," pp. 162f.

6. Mayer, *Paul Celan*, diss., pp. 16f.

7. See the *Encyclopaedia Judaica*, I (Berlin: Eschkol, 1928), cols. 38f.

8. See Peter Mayer's useful discussion of this cycle in *Paul Celan*, diss., pp. 68-73.

9. Buber, *Werke*, III, p. 552.

10. Reported by Johannes Firges in his discussion of the poem in *Die Gestaltungsschichten*, pp. 60f.

11. Rainer Maria Rilke, *Sämtliche Werke*, I (Frankfurt: Insel, 1955), p. 398.

12. Wienold, "Paul Celans," p. 226.

13. *The Complete Poetry of John Donne*, ed. John Shawcross (New York: New York University Press, 1968), p. 334. A second example is the long religious cycle *Corona benignitatis anni dei* by Paul Claudel.

14. Joseph Gaer, *The Legend of the Wandering Jew* (New York: Mentor, 1961), pp. 77f.

15. Quoted in the *Encyclopaedia Judaica*, I, col. 1151.

16. The "Christus-Visionen" had not been published at the time "Corona" was written. The significant lines had, however, been quoted from Rilke's manuscript in a scholarly work (Marianne Sievers, *Biblische Motive in der Dichtung Rainer Maria Rilkes*

[Berlin: Ebering, 1938, p. 84]). It is quite possible that Celan consulted this work; the title of Sievers's study would certainly have interested him, and he is known to have been an avid reader for whom such esoteric subjects had an especial appeal.

17. Prawer, "Paul Celan," p. 165.

18. Gershom Scholem, *Major Trends in Jewish Mysticism* (New York: Schocken, 1967), p. 239.

19. Buber, *Werke*, III, pp. 297f.

20. Kurt Bräutigam, *Moderne deutsche Balladen* (Frankfurt: Diesterweg, 1968), p. 78.

21. Hans Mayer, "Errinnerung," p. 1150.

22. T. Adorno, *Noten zur Literatur, III* (Frankfurt: Suhrkamp, 1965), p. 125. See the discussion in Walter Müller-Seidel, *Probleme der literarischen Wertung* (Stuttgart: Metzler, 1965), pp. 178-80, where an excellent refutation of this objection is given: "A poem—even a modern one—cannot be beautiful [schön] enough, as long as it palliates [beschönigt] nothing" (p. 180).

23. Wolfgang Menzel, "Celans Gedicht 'Todesfuge.' Das Paradoxon einer Fuge über den Tod in Auschwitz," *Germanisch-Romanische Monatsschrift*, NS 18 (1968), 445f.

24. L. L. Duroche, "Paul Celan's 'Todesfuge': A New Interpretation," *Modern Language Notes*, 82 (1967), 475f.

25. Dieter Lotze, "Zu Celans 'Todesfuge' im Mittelstufenunterricht," *Die Unterrichtspraxis*, 1 (1968), 75f.

26. Menzel, "Celans Gedicht 'Todesfuge,'" p. 444.

27. Dorothea Forstner, *Die Welt der Symbole*, 2nd. ed. (Innsbruck: Tyrolia, 1967), pp. 113f.; emphasis in the original.

28. *Ibid.*, p. 125.

29. *Ibid.*, pp. 306f.

30. Lotze, "Zu Celans 'Todesfuge,'" p. 76.

31. Duroche, "Paul Celan's 'Todesfuge,'" p. 476.

32. Pfullingen: Neske [1958].

33. Menzel, "Celans Gedicht 'Todesfuge,'" p. 446.

Chapter Four

1. Lyon, "Poetry of Paul Celan," p. 54.

2. Firges, *Die Gestaltungsschichten*, p. 19. The statistics relating to the frequency of the pronouns are taken from Firges, pp. 18f.

3. T. S. R. Boase, *St. Francis of Assisi* (Bloomington: Indiana University Press, 1968), p. 29.

4. *Ibid.*, p. 46.

5. See Dorothea Forstner, *Die Welt der Symbole*, p. 406.

6. Lyon, "Poetry of Paul Celan," p. 59.

7. Firges's explanation of the three as present, past, and future time (p. 128) is indicative of the failure of his generally sound study to appreciate the significance of religious language in Celan's poetry.

8. Prawer, "Paul Celan," p. 168.

9. *Der kleine Pauly,* III (Stuttgart: Druckenmüller, 1969), cols. 711 and 713.

10. Mayer, "Paul Celan," *Emuna Horizonte,* p. 190.

11. See D. Forstner, *Die Welt der Symbole,* p. 135.

12. Lyon, "Nature. Its Idea and Use," p. 141.

13. Prawer, "Paul Celan," p. 177.

14. Many critics have discussed this poem. See especially Peter Mayer, *Paul Celan,* diss., p. 87; Johannes Firges, "Sprache und Sein," pp. 262-64; Norbert Johannimloh, "Paul Celan, 'Mit wechselndem Schlüssel,'" *Der Deutschunterricht,* 17, 4, (1965), 76-81; and Silvio Vietta, *Sprache und Sprachreflexion in der modernen Lyrik* (Bad Homburg: Gehlen, 1970), pp. 99-101.

15. Firges offers the following interpretation of this passage: "The word is the key to this house" ("Sprache und Sein," p. 263), and critics, perhaps following his lead, interpret the "word" to be the key to Celan's poetry; cf. Vietta's comment on this poem: "Language moves into the center of the poetical process" (p. 100). Such is not the case, in the present poem or in general. Emotion, based on past experiences and present attitudes, is invariably the key to Celan's poetry.

16. This important poem has not been the subject of a detailed interpretation. The most extensive treatment can be found in Lyon's dissertation, pp. 110 and 197.

17. Mayer, "Paul Celan," *Emuna Horizonte,* p. 190.

18. Cf. Lyon's interpretation of "Mit Äxten spieland," in "Poetry of Paul Celan," pp. 61f.

19. The most extensive discussion of this poem is given in Beda Allemann's "Nachwort" to P. Celan, *Ausgewählte Gedichte* (Frankfurt: Suhrkamp, 1968), pp. 151f.; see also the interesting treatment by H. G. Kaern, "Der Lyriker Paul Celan: Untersuchung seiner Symbolik und Sprache" (diss., Nebraska, 1970), pp. 71f. and 173-75.

Chapter Five

1. Alfred Kelletat, "Accessus," *Über Paul Celan,* ed. Dietlind Meinecke (Frankfurt: Suhrkamp, 1970), pp. 116f.

2. "Stimmen" has been interpreted by Klaus Weissenberger, *Die Elegie bei Paul Celan* (Berne: Francke, 1969), pp. 41f.

3. It is also one of the most frequently interpreted poems; see

especially Weissenberger, pp. 47f. and Peter Mayer, *Paul Celan,* diss., pp. 94f.

4. Hans Mayer, *Zur deutschen Literatur der Zeit* (Reinbek: Rowohlt, 1967), pp. 357-59; and "Erinnerung," pp. 1158f.

5. Walter Jens, "Nüchternheit und Präzision im Hymnos," *Über Paul Celan,* pp. 50f.

6. Peter Horst Neumann, "Wortnacht und Augennacht," *Neue Rundschau,* 79 (1968), 88-99; I follow Neumann's astute interpretation in many respects.

7. Wienold, "Paul Celans," pp. 216-28.

8. Prawer draws this parallel in his "Paul Celan," p. 173.

9. Ruth Lorbe, "Paul Celan, 'Tenebrae,' " *Über Paul Celan,* p. 249. I follow Lorbe's study in several other points of interpretation.

10. I described some aspects of the "Widerruf" in my article "Celan's Transformation of Benn's 'Südwort': An Interpretation of the poem 'Sprachgitter,' " *German Life & Letters,* NS 21 (1967-68), 11-17, which the present interpretation follows in some respects. Several other detailed interpretations of the poem have been published.

11. Benn, *Gesammelte Werke,* I, pp. 511f.

12. Kelletat, p. 197, mentions the relevance of the second verse to "Sprachgitter," citing a word play in the poem.

13. Benn, *Werke,* III, p. 263.

14. Joachim Schulze, "Mystische Motive in Paul Celans Gedichten," *Poetica,* 3 (1970), 506f., names a further source, Martin Buber's metaphor "Lifting the eyelids in silence."

15. Lyon, "Poetry of Paul Celan," p. 59.

16. Benn, *Werke,* III, p. 208.

17. Hanna Vogt, *Joch und Krone* (Frankfurt: Ner-Tamed, 1963), pp. 7-9.

18. Mayer, *Paul Celan,* diss., p. 88.

Chapter Six

1. Dietlind Meinecke reports that Celan once explained the dedication as a memorial for those "who have borne the fate of poets [*die Dichterisches getragen haben*]," *Wort und Name bei Paul Celan* (Bad Homburg: Gehlen, 1970), p. 167; Celan's statement cannot be taken at face value. He was undoubtedly making a veiled ironic reference to the motto of another of his poems, "All poets are Jews," since *Die Niemandsrose*—unlike *Von Schwelle zu Schwelle* or even *Sprachgitter*—obviously commemorates Jews, and not poets.

2. Prawer refers to the connection between the two poems in "Paul Celan," pp. 166f.

3. Rubenstein, *After Auschwitz,* p. 153.

4. Beda Allemann, *Die Neue Rundschau*, 75 (1964), 148.

5. Cf. Hans-Jürgen Heise, "Nach Paul Celans Tod," *Neue deutsche Hefte*, 17, 3 (1970), 100-114, especially 103f.; Heise, like many critics, prefers the concise texts of *Sprachgitter* to those of *Die Niemandsrose* with their "stale romantic vocabulary." I do not share this value judgment; the rhythmical effects and skillfully placed repetitions of *Die Niemandsrose*, together with the personal and highly emotional subject matter, produce poems of remarkable quality.

6. Olof Lagercrantz, "Die fortdauernde Schöpfung," *Text + Kritik*, No. 23 (1969), pp. 2f.

7. Prawer, "Paul Celan," p. 178.

8. Mayer, *Paul Celan*, diss., pp. 70f.

9. Milo Dor, "Paul Celan," *Über Paul Celan*, ed. D. Meinecke (Frankfurt, Suhrkamp, 1970), pp. 284f.

10. See the convincingly argued interpretation by Klaus Weissenberger in *Die Elegie bei Paul Celan* (Berne: Francke, 1969), pp. 64-68.

11. Mayer, *Paul Celan*, diss., p. 119; Meinecke, *Wort und Name*, pp. 164f. See also Peter Horst Neumann's useful interpretation of the poem, *Zur Lyrik Paul Celans* (Göttingen: Vandenhoeck and Ruprecht, 1968), pp. 34f.

12. Rubenstein, *After Auschwitz*, p. 152.

13. See the interpretations by Martin Anderle, "Die Zeit im Gedicht," *German Quarterly*, 44 (1971), 495f., and Peter Mayer, *Paul Celan*, diss., pp. 151f.

14. Cf. Conrad Moehlman, *The Christian-Jewish Tragedy*, pp. 150f.

15. Meinecke, *Wort und Name*, p. 135.

16. See Hans Mayer's remarks on this subject in "Erinnerung," pp. 1153f. The usually astute Mayer errs in referring to passages from "Und mit dem Buch aus Tarussa" and "In der Luft" as though they constituted a single long poem, thereby rendering his conclusions less reliable than they might have been.

17. The first detailed, and still the best, formulation of this view is given by Peter Paul Schwarz, *Totengedächtnis und dialogische Polarität in der Lyrik Paul Celans* (Düsseldorf: Schwann, 1966), pp. 51-53.

18. See especially the carefully argued study of Joachim Schulze, "Mystische Motive in Paul Celans Gedichten," *Poetica*, 3 (1970), 484-95. Although I am indebted to Schulze's fine study, I do not agree with his conclusions. He, for example, denies even the negative implications of "Tenebrae" (p. 489) and interprets "Psalm" and "Mandorla" as poems of affirmation. I would interpret the numerous

allusions in these poems to religious sources to be for the most part ironic, as with "Tenebrae."

19. The transition is not nearly as natural and unforced in English as it is in German. Cf. Odysseus's use of a similar word play in the *Odyssey*.

20. William Rey, "Das blühende Nichts," *German Quarterly*, 43 (1970), 761.

21. Schwarz, *Totengedächtnis*, p. 52; Ernst Kostal, "Paul Celan zwischen Nihilismus und metaphysischer Spekulation," *Literatur und Kritik*, No. 52 (1971), p. 108.

22. See Schulze, "Mystische Motive," p. 494.

23. Wiesel, *Legends of our Time*, p. 61.

24. The present interpretation is largely taken from my article "Manifestations of the Holocaust: Interpreting Paul Celan," *Books Abroad*," 46 (1972), 25-30.

25. See Wolfgang Binder, *Das Bild des Menschen in der modernen deutschen Literatur* (Zürich: Artemis, 1969), p. 34.

26. For a discussion of the mystical concept "God as Nothingness" see especially Schulze, "Mystische Motive," pp. 473-84, and Gerhard Neumann, "Die 'absolute' Metapher. Ein Abgrenzungsversuch am Beispiel Stéphane Mallarmés und Paul Celans," *Poetica*, 3 (1970), 211-15.

27. Werner Weber, *Tagebuch eines Lesers* (Olten: Walter, 1965), p. 87.

28. Peter Mayer, *Paul Celan*, diss., pp. 156f., mentions the parallel to "Espenbaum" yet emphasizes the aspect of eternity in his interpretation.

29. Wiesel, *Night*, p. 91.

30. Compare the treatments of the dilemma by Elie Wiesel, "Appointment with Hate," pp. 165-78, and "A Plea for the Dead," pp. 215-37, in *Legends of our Time*; and by Friedrich Torberg in *Mein ist die Rache* (Los Angeles: Pazifische Presse, 1943).

Chapter Seven

1. Christoph Perels, "Das Gedicht im Exil," *Über Paul Celan*, ed. D. Meinecke (Frankfurt: Suhrkamp, 1970), p. 212.

2. Weissenberger, *Die Elegie*, p. 78.

3. H. G. Gadamer, "Des Dichters wahres Wort," *Neue Zürcher Zeitung*, January 17, 1971, pp. 49f. Some of my discussion is based on this interesting article.

4. Weissenberger, *Die Elegie*, pp. 70f.

5. This poem has been discussed by several critics; in addition to Gadamer, see especially P. H. Neumann, *Zur Lyrik*, pp. 80f., and Weissenberger, pp. 72f.

6. Mayer, *Paul Celan,* diss., p. 201; Jürgen P. Wallmann, "Paul Celan," *Argumente* (Mühlacker: Stieglitz, 1968), p. 151.

7. Wilhelm Höck, "Von welchem Gott ist die Rede?" *Über Paul Celan,* p. 274.

Chapter Eight

1. Joachim Günther, *Neue deutsche Hefte,* No. 120 (1968), pp. 126-29.

2. Hans Mayer, "Erinnerung," p. 1159.

3. See the interpretation by Werner Weber, "Zum Gedicht 'Du sei wie du,'" *Über Paul Celan,* ed. D. Meinecke (Frankfurt: Suhrkamp, 1970), pp. 277-80.

4. See the short but useful discussions of Alvin Rosenfeld, "Poetry and Violence," *European Judaism,* 4, 2 (1970), 45-47; and Meinecke, *Wort und Name,* pp. 62-64.

5. See the valuable interpretation of Joachim Schulze, "Mystische Motive," pp. 502f.

Chapter Nine

1. Hermann Hakel, ed., *Die Bibel im deutschen Gedicht,* 2nd. ed. (Munich: Kindler, 1968), p. 706.

2. "Poems, Noems," *Times Literary Supplement,* December 7, 1967, p. 1190.

Selected Bibliography

A thorough bibliography of Celan's works, translations of his works, and critical studies about him has been compiled and edited by Dietlind Meinecke, *Über Paul Celan* (Frankfurt: Suhrkamp, 1970), pp. 291-319.

PRIMARY SOURCES

1. Books of Poetry

Der Sand aus den Urnen. With lithographs by Edgar Jené. Vienna: Sexl, 1948.
Mohn und Gedächtnis. Stuttgart: Deutsche Verlags-Anstalt, 1952.
Von Schwelle zu Schwelle. Stuttgart: Deutsche Verlags-Anstalt, 1955.
Sprachgitter. Frankfurt: S. Fischer, 1959.
Die Niemandsrose. Frankfurt: S. Fischer, 1963.
Atemkristall. With etchings by Gisèle Celan-Lestrange. Paris: Brunidor, 1965. Limited edition.
Atemwende. Frankfurt: Suhrkamp, 1967.
Todtnauberg. Paris: Brunidor, 1968. Limited edition.
Fadensonnen. Frankfurt: Suhrkamp, 1968.
Schwarzmaut. With etchings by Gisèle Celan-Lestrange. Paris: Brunidor, 1969.
Lichtzwang. Frankfurt: Suhrkamp, 1970.
Schneepart. Frankfurt: Suhrkamp, 1971.

2. Translations

JEAN COCTEAU, *Der goldene Vorhang. Brief an die Amerikaner.* Bad Salzig: Rauch, 1949.
ALEXANDER BLOCK, *Die Zwölf.* Frankfurt: S. Fischer, 1958.
ARTHUR RIMBAUD, *Das trunkene Schiff.* Wiesbaden: Insel, 1958.
OSIP MANDELSHTAM. *Gedichte.* Frankfurt: S. Fischer, 1959.
PAUL VALÉRY, *Die junge Parze.* Wiesbaden: Insel, 1960. Limited edition.
SERGEI JESSENIN, *Gedichte.* Frankfurt: S. Fischer, 1961.
JEAN CAYROL, *Im Bereich einer Nacht.* Olten: Walter, 1961.
WILLIAM SHAKESPEARE, *Einundzwanzig Sonette.* Frankfurt: Insel, 1967.
JULES SUPERVIELLE, *Gedichte.* Frankfurt: Insel, 1968.
ANDRÉ DU BOUCHET, *Vakante Glut.* Frankfurt: Suhrkamp, 1968.

Giuseppe Ungaretti, *Das verheißene Land. Das Merkbuch des Alten.* Frankfurt: Insel, 1968.
(See Meinecke's bibliography for a list of translations which have appeared in periodicals and anthologies.)

3. Prose Fiction

"Gespräch im Gebirg." *Die Neue Rundschau,* 71 (1960), pp. 199-202. Reprinted in Paul Celan, *Ausgewählte Gedichte,* ed. Klaus Reichert (Frankfurt: Suhrkamp, 1970), pp. 181-86.

4. Other Important Prose

"Edgar Jené und der Traum vom Traume." *Edgar Jené. Der Traum vom Traume.* Vienna: Agathon, 1948, pp. 7-12.
"Rede anläßlich der Entgegennahme des Literaturpreises der Freien Hansestadt Bremen." *Ansprachen bei Verleihung des Bremer Literaturpreises an Paul Celan.* Stuttgart: Deutsche Verlags-Anstalt, n.d. Reprinted in Paul Celan, *Ausgewählte Gedichte,* ed. Beda Allemann (Frankfurt: Suhrkamp, 1968), pp. 127-29.
[Short text on his poetic work]. *Almanach der librairie Flinker 1958.* Paris: La Librairie Française et Etrangère, 1958, p. 45. Reprinted in *Über Paul Celan,* ed. Dietlind Meinecke (Frankfurt: Suhrkamp, 1970), p. 23.
[Letter to Hans Bender, dated May 18, 1960]. *Mein Gedicht ist mein Messer,* ed. H. Bender. 2nd. ed. Munich: List, 1961, pp. 86f. Reprinted in *Über Paul Celan,* ed. Dietlind Meinecke (Frankfurt: Suhrkamp, 1970), pp. 26f.
Der Meridian. Frankfurt: S. Fischer, 1961. Also in *Jahrbuch der Deutschen Akademie für Sprache und Dichtung 1960.* Heidelberg: Lambert Schneider, 1961, pp. 74-88; and, slightly abridged in Paul Celan, *Ausgewählte Gedichte,* ed. Beda Allemann (Frankfurt: Suhrkamp, 1968), pp. 131-48.
[Letter to Robert Neumann]. *34 x erste Liebe,* ed. Robert Neumann (Frankfurt: Barmeier & Nikel, 1966), pp. 32f.

5. Selection of Poems in English Translation

Speech-Grille. Trans. Joachim Neugröschel. New York: E. P. Dutton and Co., 1971. Contains all the poems of *Sprachgitter* and selections from the remaining collections; a dual language book.

SECONDARY SOURCES

(Not including material relating to specific works or problems and listed in the notes to the various chapters of the present

study. Many additional references can be found in Dietlind
Meinecke's bibliography.)

ALLEMANN, BEDA. "Paul Celan." *Schriftsteller der Gegegenwart*, ed.
Klaus Nonnenmann. Olten: Walter, 1963, pp. 70-75.

ANDERLE, MARTIN. "Strukturlinien in der Lyrik Paul Celans." *Wort
in der Zeit*, 12 (1960), 19-25.

BASIL, OTTO. "Wir leben unter finsteren Himmeln." *Literatur und
Kritik*. No. 52 (1971), pp. 102-05.

BUCH, WILFRIED. "Paul Celan: 'Espenbaum,' 'Todesfuge,' 'Die
Krüge.'" *Kristalle*, ed. Josef Speck. Munich: Kösel, 1967, pp.
174-88.

BUTZLAFF, WOLFGANG and PETER SEIDENSTICKER. "Zwei Bemühungen
um ein Gedicht ['Todesfuge']." *Der Deutschunterricht*, 12, 3
(1960), 34-51.

Études Germaniques, 25, 3 (1970). Special issue of the periodical
entirely devoted to Celan.

FIRGES, JOHANNES. *Die Gestaltungsschichten in der Lyrik Paul Celans
ausgehend vom Wortmaterial*. Dissertation, Cologne, 1959.

--------. "Sprache und Sein in der Dichtung Paul Celans," *Muttersprache*, 72 (1962), 261-69.

FORSTER, LEONARD. "'Espenbaum.' Zu einem Gedicht von Paul
Celan." *Wissenschaft als Dialog*, ed. R. v. Heydebrandt and
K. G. Just. Stuttgart: Metzler, 1969, pp. 380-85.

HEISE, HANS-JÜRGEN. "Nach Paul Celans Tod." *Neue deutsche Hefte*,
17, 3 (1970), 100-114.

JASPERSEN, URSULA. "'Todesfuge' von Paul Celan." *Begegnung mit
Gedichten*, ed. Walter Urbanek. Bamberg: Buchners, 1967, pp.
268-73.

JOKOSTRA, PETER. "Zeit und Unzeit in der Dichtung Paul Celans."
Eckart, 29 (1960), 162-74.

KAERN, HEINZ GEORG. "Der Lyriker Paul Celan: Untersuchung seiner
Symbolik und Sprache." Dissertation, Nebraska, 1970.

KELLETAT, ALFRED. "Accessus zu Celans 'Sprachgitter.'" *Über Paul
Celan*, ed. Dietlind Meinecke (Frankfurt: Suhrkamp, 1970),
pp. 113-37.

KIM, DOROTEA. *Paul Celan als Dichter der Bewahrung. Versuch
einer Interpretation*. Aarau: Sauerländer, 1969 (also dissertation, Zurich, 1969).

LYON, JAMES K. "Nature. Its Idea and Use in the Poetic Imagery of
Ingeborg Bachmann, Paul Celan, and Karl Krolow." Dissertation,
Harvard, 1962.

--------. "Paul Celan and Martin Buber: Poetry as Dialogue." *PMLA*,
86 (1971), 110-20.

––––––. "The Poetry of Paul Celan: An Approach." *Germanic Review*, 39 (1964), 50-67.

MAYER, HANS. "Erinnerung an Paul Celan." *Merkur*, 24 (1970), 1150-63.

MAYER, PETER. *Paul Celan als jüdischer Dichter*. Dissertation, Heidelberg, 1969.

––––––. "Paul Celan als jüdischer Dichter." *Emuna Horizonte*, 5 (1970), 190-95.

MEINECKE, DIETLIND. *Wort und Name bei Paul Celan*. Bad Homburg: Gehlen, 1970.

MÜLLER, HARTMUT. *Formen moderner deutscher Lyrik*. Paderborn: Schöningh, 1970.

NEUMANN, GERHARD. "Die 'absolute' Metapher. Ein Abgrenzungsversuch am Beispiel Stéphane Mallarmés und Paul Celans." *Poetica*, 3 (1970), 188-225.

NEUMANN, PETER HORST. *Wort-Konkordanz zur Lyrik Paul Celans*. Munich: Fink, 1969.

––––––. *Zur Lyrik Paul Celans*. Göttingen: Vandenhoeck & Ruprecht, 1968.

OPPENS, KURT. "Gesang und Magie im Zeitalter des Steins. Zur Dichtung Ingeborg Bachmanns und Paul Celans." *Merkur*, 17 (1963), 175-93.

PRAWER, SIEGBERT. "Paul Celan." *Essays on Contemporary German Literature*, ed. Brian Keith-Smith. London: O. Wolff, 1966, pp. 161-84.

REY, WILLIAM. "Paul Celan: Das blühende Nichts." *German Quarterly*, 43 (1970), 749-69.

SCHULZE, JOACHIM. "Mystische Motive in Paul Celans Gedichten." *Poetica*, 3 (1970), 472-509.

SCHWARZ, PETER PAUL. *Totengedächtnis und dialogische Polarität in der Lyrik Paul Celans*. Düsseldorf: Schwann, 1966.

SZONDI, PETER. "Poetry of constancy—Poetik der Beständigkeit. Celans Übertragung von Shakespeare Sonett 105." *Sprache im technischen Zeitalter*, No. 37 (1971), pp. 9-25.

Über Paul Celan, ed. DIETLIND MEINECKE. Frankfurt: Suhrkamp, 1970. Contains a representative sample of articles on Celan from 1952 to 1970, as well as two original contributions and a detailed bibliography.

WALLMANN, JÜRGEN. "Paul Celan—sein Weg und seine Dichtung." *Universitas*, 26 (1971), 33-47.

WEISSENBERGER, KLAUS. *Die Elegie bei Paul Celan*. Berne: Francke, 1969.

WIENOLD, GÖTZ. "Paul Celans Hölderlin-Widerruf." *Poetica*, 2 (1968), 216-28.

Index

(Includes first references in the notes to investigators when the cited work does not appear in the Selected Bibliography.)

171

90170